LIFE
Is a
GIFT

LIFE
Is a
GIFT

INSPIRATION FROM THE
SOON DEPARTED

Bob and Judy Fisher

New York   Boston   Nashville

Unless otherwise indicated, Scriptures are taken from the New American Standard Bible®, Copyright © 1960, 1962, 1963, 1968, 1972, 1975, 1977, 1995 by The Lockman Foundation. Used by permission.

Scriptures noted NIV are taken from the HOLY BIBLE: NEW INTERNATIONAL VERSION® Copyright © 1973, 1978, 1984 by International Bible Society. Used by permission of Zondervan Publishing House. All rights reserved.

Scriptures noted NLT are from the *Holy Bible*, New Living Translation, Copyright © 1996. Used by permission of Tyndale House Publishers, Inc., Wheaton, Illinois 60189. All rights reserved.

Scriptures noted KJV are taken from the King James Version of the Bible.

Scriptures noted NKJV are taken from the NEW KING JAMES VERSION. Copyright © 1979, 1980, 1982, Thomas Nelson, Inc., Publishers.

FaithWords
Hachette Book Group USA
237 Park Avenue
New York, NY 10017

Visit our Web site at www.faithwords.com.

Printed in the United States of America

First Edition: May 2008

10 9 8 7 6 5 4 3 2 1

FaithWords is a division of Hachette Book Group USA, Inc.
The FaithWords name and logo are trademarks of Hachette Book Group USA, Inc.

Library of Congress Cataloging-in-Publication Data
Fisher, Bob.
  Life is a gift : inspiration from the soon departed / Bob and Judy Fisher. — 1st ed.
    p. cm.
  ISBN-13: 978-0-446-19636-9
  ISBN-10: 0-446-19636-3
  1. Terminally ill—Religious life. 2. Death—Religious aspects—Christianity.
I. Fisher, Judy. II. Title.
  BV4910.F58 2008
  248.8'6175—dc22   2007030666

Book design by Charles Sutherland

Dedicated to what really matters—our family

Rob
Kelly and Ben
Jennifer and Neil and the boys—Josh, Sam, Ben, and Jacob

And

Inspired by the lives of Adam and David

"Before I draw nearer to that stone to
which you point, answer me one question.
Are these the shadows of the things that Will be,
or
are they shadows of the things that May be only?"

(Ebenezer Scrooge questions
"The Ghost of Christmas Yet To Come"
as they approach Scrooge's tombstone.)
A Christmas Carol, Charles Dickens

CONTENTS

ACKNOWLEDGMENTS

Writing this book has been one of the most wonderful experiences of our lives. And, as we make clear in our writing, the greatest wonders of life are people. The people who have enabled this book comprise a long and diverse list. First, there is Sue Heflin who has been so helpful at every step along the way, helping to balance day-to-day work with a vision for this book. Ana Cesmat was remarkable in her ability to transcribe the interview tapes, even to the point of reflecting the tone of voice.

This book would not be completed today without the great skill and good effort of Jonathan Rogers who served in the critical roles of organizer, assembler, and pre-submission editor. In fact, the reader can probably discern that this is the only page Jonathan did not have the opportunity to review and revise.

Alive Hospice of Nashville was the inspiration and the vehicle for our work. Pam Brown was relentless in working with us for almost four years as she coordinated the connection between our efforts and the lives of the 104 people we interviewed. Jan Jones, the CEO of Alive Hospice, was supportive and encouraging at every turn.

Additional thank-yous are due to Dr. John Sergent and Dr.

Roy Elam at Vanderbilt University Hospital for their support and encouragement of this effort. These two are making a difference in hospice and palliative care. The influence of our pastor, Dr. Frank Lewis, shows through in whatever is judged to be positive in our work.

I would also like to acknowledge that the initial spark for the idea behind the book was generated many years ago in a late-night conversation with my friend and colleague Dr. Bo Thomas. I must also admit that our relationship has so shaped my thinking that I can't remember which stories and ideas are mine and which are his.

The editorial staff at FaithWords has been wonderful. I am especially thankful for Gary Terashita and Cara Highsmith for their professional attitude and for blending that into friendship.

In every project it takes someone to bring everyone together. For this project, it was Bucky Rosenbaum, our agent, who brought us all together, and then kept us together. Our divinely inspired appointment has brought great joy to our work.

We received a priceless gift from the 104 people who, along with their families, participated in these conversations. As we talked with them we developed a tentative title around the concept that they "would soon depart" this earth. By the time we were in the writing stages, they had "already departed." These people revealed to us with transparency and trust what really matters to them. Most of them let us see deep into their being. They have changed our lives. We hope you will listen carefully to what they have to say—they have the potential to change your life as well.

INTRODUCTION

William E. is a logger—or at least he had been. He had always been a physically powerful man, always taking pride in his ability to outwork anybody in the woodlot. But the robust logger's eyes now reflected that he was a man who lay dying of cancer.

Even as William's physical self wasted away, however, he learned to see things he'd missed when he was still able to place confidence in the flesh. Things that once seemed important were now off his radar screen entirely, and little things—little moments of being fully present, tiny opportunities to connect with another human being—now were to William life itself.

"I believe you ought to tell people how you feel about them—straight up—even the bad, while you can," William told us. "Look at someone and tell them you love them. Tell them every chance you can that you love them. If you don't love them, try to understand and get along, and then try to love them." This from a man who never considered himself very wise, a man who always avoided "brain work," as he called it. But now his brain—and his heart—were working hard to make sense of a life nearing its end.

"Don't take the small stuff for granted," William said. "And give all you can to others. Give it all and don't take nothing for granted. If a child smiles at you, smile back and know that you've just had a good day. If someone shakes your hand, hang on to their hand for just an instant longer than they expect."

To whom do you go to find the meaning of life? Through most of his forty-odd years, William wouldn't have seemed an obvious choice. He wasn't very educated. He made his share of bad choices. He devoted his energies not to solving the problems of the world, but to chains and skidders and staying out of the way of falling trees. And yet, there at the end of his life, he spoke with the terse wisdom of a swami of the joy in receiving a smile from a child and the importance of shaking hands longer than usual. There's a whole worldview there, an entire philosophy of human relationships.

William was one of 104 dying people we interviewed to make this book. They were patients of Alive Hospice in Nashville, Tennessee. Most were old; some were quite young (including a five-year-old). Some were in grievous pain when we talked to them; some were in the fog of powerful pain-killing drugs; a few looked healthy enough on the outside, even while they were being ravaged by disease on the inside. Some were rural, some urban, some from the leafy suburbs. They came from every socio-economic stratum. After all, nothing is so democratic as death. They all had one thing in common, however: each accepted looming death as an unavoidable fact. They were all beyond the help of modern medicine; to be admitted into hospice care a patient must sign a document stating he or she has decided not to seek life-saving (or life-prolonging) treatments and his or her prognosis is six months or less to live. Some of the 104 died within days of talking with us. None of them are alive today.

A few of our interviewees spoke, like William, in quotable little chestnuts of wisdom. More often, however, their wisdom came out in choices they made in their dying days, in a new way of seeing the world that was too all-encompassing to make its way into a one-liner. Over and over again, we talked to people who exuded wisdom they didn't know they had—extraordinary people who thought of themselves as very ordinary.

There was the ninety-eight-year-old man who was learning Hungarian. It was something he always wanted to do. The fact that he only had a few weeks to live didn't discourage him from the task, but rather served as a motivation to stop putting it off.

There was Beverly, who sold off some of the stock that was supposed to be her children's inheritance and rented a beach house so she and her children and grandchildren could make another week of memories together. She had sense enough to know the truest heritage she could give her children couldn't be tallied on a brokerage statement.

There was five-year-old Maddie, who reminded us of the importance of living in the present and grabbing hold of every pleasure life offers. "When the sun is out there, I'm happy," she said.

Our conversations for the most part followed a standard question-and-answer formula. We asked a few simple questions: *What are you most proud of? What has been your greatest joy? What has been your greatest disappointment? What's the most important thing you've ever done? What do you regret? What comes next for you? If you could give one message to the world, what would it be?*

Simple questions—not easy questions. It wasn't always comfortable to put people on the spot in their dying days. So why did we do it? Because we wanted to glean the wisdom of those who are "near-to-death." Death's approach has a way of focusing people—allowing them to see truths hidden in plain sight. You've heard stories of people who have a near-death experience and change their way of thinking about the world. They realize life is precious, and they resolve not to waste any more of it. In talking to the soon-departed, it was our goal to have an experience of being "near-to-death" and to see where it led us.

It's no easy thing to think through the most important questions of life and death when you're caught up in the whirl of the everyday. Hospice patients are in a unique position: they are still in the land of the living, and yet all the trivialities and false urgencies of the living have been burned away. When you're barely hanging on to life, it's hard to hang on to things like petty jealousy and greed and bitterness.

It's not that the dying possess supernatural wisdom. To be honest, some of the people we spoke with weren't very wise at all. But each of them, since coming face-to-face with death, thought more about what really matters in life than they ever had before.

We as a culture think about death as little as possible. We prefer to focus on the positive. Unless death is staring us in the face, why even think about it? Why not just cross that bridge when we come to it?

Actually, there are grave dangers in refusing to face the

fact of our mortality. When we view life as if it were an in-exhaustible resource, we tend to waste it. We major on the minors. We leave crucial things undone.

Behind the questions we asked the patients of Alive Hospice were other questions we were asking ourselves: *How can the living benefit from the wisdom of the dying? How will it change us to be confronted with death while we are still healthy and thriving? What would happen if we confronted others with the same experience?*

There was a tradition in the art and culture of medieval and Renaissance Europe known as memento mori—"reminder of death." Artists and craftsmen worked images of skulls and skeletons into paintings, jewelry, wall hangings, and stained glass. It sounds morbid—and in many cases it was—but the point was to create a world in which people were constantly reminded that this life is short, that every day counts. This book, you might say, is our memento mori. It is our hope to remind the reader—just as we reminded ourselves—that this life is short, and every day counts.

The themes that emerged in our conversations probably won't surprise anyone. Family. Faith. Forgiveness. Gratitude. An appreciation for small blessings. A willingness to live in the present rather than dwelling on the past or fretting about the future. We heard a lot about God and heaven and leaving it all behind. We heard that death is healing and we observed the fearlessness with which almost all of these people faced the end of their lives on earth. We heard laughter in the face of death and came to understand the importance of laughter in life. Most universally, we heard that what matters most in life are relationships with children, parents, grandchildren, spouses, friends, and God.

The nuggets we mined mostly fall into the category that our friend Tom Stuart called "remember what you know." He taught our Bible study, and he ended every lesson with the same exhortation: "Remember what you know!" Most of us already know what we need to know to live a fulfilling life. What we really need is the courage, motivation, and faith to act on what we already know to be true.

As you read this book, in many cases you may tell yourself, "I already knew that." This isn't rocket science. But for us, what was life changing about our "near-to-death" experiences were the stories of courage, motivation, and faith we heard. Our hope is you, too, will find courage, motivation, and faith to live out the things you already know to be true. You will find that a recurring theme in the following conversations is regret—so many of our interviewees realized too late there was a significant gap between the things they knew they ought to be doing and the things they actually did. For you, however, it's probably not too late. Our ultimate hope for this book is that the unique insights and inspirational courage of these 104 people cause you to remember what you know and encourage you in a life with no regrets.

LIFE
Is a
GIFT

Chapter 1

THE BLESSINGS OF EARTH

We saw a lot of joy in the hospice rooms and death beds we visited—more joy than you might expect. A lot of it rose from the fact these were people who were just glad to be alive. They didn't take any day for granted. James A. told us his greatest joy was "being alive," and he meant it. He was grateful for the life he lived—in spite of the mistakes he made, in spite of his humble circumstances. "I'm just proud of my life," he said. "There's some people that wouldn't be, but that doesn't make any difference to me."

Given the pain these people were facing, the uncertainty, the sadness of leaving everything behind, you would think it would take a lot—a lottery win, a trip to Paris, a Nobel Prize—to overcome all that and give them joy. But that's not what we observed. Our interviewees found joy in the things that had been there all along. Reitha was pretty typical: she told us her greatest joy was simply being pain-free and having her family together.

The hope of heaven gave people a lot of joy (we'll delve into that in another chapter), but the people we interviewed had also learned how to enjoy the blessings of *this* life. There was a palpable tension for many of our interviewees: they eagerly looked forward to heaven, but they couldn't help mourning at least a little for the good and blessed life they were leaving behind.

George said, "My only regret? I'm not gonna be able to live as long as I would like to. I hate to leave." George believed he was going to a better place. But who could blame him for being sad to leave? "I have a very good life," he said. "I've married a beautiful woman, have three real fine boys and nine grandchildren."

George was like Lucy at the end of *The Last Battle*, the final book in C. S. Lewis's *The Chronicles of Narnia*. She was standing on the front porch of heaven—the New Narnia—reunited with all her friends and family, in the presence of Aslan (the Christ figure of Narnia), yet she cried to see the door closed on the old Narnia. Her brother Peter scolded her:

> "What, Lucy! You're not *crying*? With Aslan ahead, and all of us here?"
>
> "Don't try to stop me, Peter," said Lucy. "I am sure Aslan would not. I am sure it is not wrong to mourn for Narnia. Think of all that lies dead and frozen behind that door."[1]

Maxine looked forward to heaven, too, but she stated her love of this life even more strongly than George did. She joked, "I think when God is ready to take me, I might pitch a fit, because I don't want to go. It's leaving your family. I have wonderful kids, grandchildren, great-grandchildren— I've seen a lot with them but I'd like to see more. . . . I'm very proud of my children and my whole family. I hate to leave them. I believe my heaven has been right here on earth. Isn't that fantastic? I'll take it."

It is truly a blessing to have lived a life you hate to leave, even when you have heaven to look forward to.

That's the irony of the situation our interviewees found themselves in. Nobody wants a slow and painful death. And yet a lingering death is what gave these people the opportunity to understand how blessed they had been. And it was a spur to their loved ones to love them the way they should have been loving all along.

Consider Mildred M. Her son's devotion to her was truly touching, and obviously a source of deep joy for her. He lived out of town, but he came to spend a week at his mother's bedside. "If I went to sleep," Mildred said, "when I woke up he'd be sitting there looking at me. He's not a talker." She smiled to think of that fifty-year-old man, sitting there gazing at his dying mother. What a beautiful image. It's such a tender, intimate moment it feels strange to write about it, almost as if it's a violation of their privacy. But it illustrates the intensity with which the dying experience life.

Shakespeare's Sonnet 73 is one of his "deathbed sonnets." It's about the intensity, the distillation of experience that results from realizing you don't have long to live. That realization, according to Shakespeare,

> *which makes thy love more strong,*
> *To love that well which thou must leave ere long.*[2]

Loving well what we must leave before long. That's one of the great themes to emerge from our interviews with hospice patients. Mildred loved her children with a new intensity, and they loved her in kind. I suppose there's no real surprise there. But she also loved life's smallest pleasures with a renewed intensity—watching Westerns on television, watching her birdfeeder out the window. "This morning there was the prettiest big redbird out there," she said, her eyes twinkling. A redbird is common enough; it may not seem worth remarking on. But what about a redbird that might be the last one you'll ever see?

In our conversations we saw the return of childlike wonder. The first redbird you see as a child—that's a miracle. Soon, however, you realize how common redbirds are, and they don't seem so miraculous . . . until you realize you're running out of redbirds. You learn again to love well what you must leave before long.

Susan was seventy-nine years old and dying of stomach cancer. But she was still in touch with the wonder and gratitude she experienced as a girl: "Once many years ago when I was eleven, I'd throw open the windows and it was so beautiful. And I said, 'Oh God, I'm so glad to be alive. Thank You.' Now I'm many years in between, and I haven't forgotten."

When it comes to what really matters to people facing death, nothing even comes close to being as important as people. We asked each of our interviewees, "What are you most proud of?" and "What brings you the greatest joy in life?" Overwhelmingly, their responses were related to people, and mainly family—wives, husbands, children, grandchildren, and so on.

Johnny said he was proudest of his grandkids, friends, and kids. "When I talk to them and see their faces, I know what I have accomplished." His greatest joy? "Recently, on a visit with my grandchildren, my eight-year-old spent eight hours on my knee telling me about what she had done that day. It meant so much to me to spend time with her."

While there were plenty of marriages that didn't work out, most did, and those involved obtained much joy, strength, and courage from their relationships. Sam said the most important thing he's ever done was "to marry my wife." He went on to say, "That sounds facetious, but it isn't. That was the greatest adventure and the greatest fun that I had in my lifetime. I'm convinced that she was made to be my wife. I don't think there's any doubt about that. My greatest joy has been living sixty-five years with the greatest woman ever made. She was such a dear soul. Couldn't have been a more perfect wife, mother, lover, and friend. What more can I say?"

Chester was a man of few, but powerful words. When we asked, *"What comes next for you?"* he answered, "Hug my wife as much as I can."

As we began our conversation with Rodney and his wife, Dena, he put one condition on his cooperation with our work: "You don't have nearly enough time to listen to all of our stories, but if you write anything about us the one thing you have to write is how much love we have between us." When Rodney told his love story with Dena, his enthusiasm spilled over in a multiplication of "very's": "It's a very, very, very special relationship that we have. . . . We've been in love since the fourth grade."

"Sixth grade," Dena corrected him.

"Well, I fell in love with you when I was in the sixth grade [Dena was in the fourth] and it took me two years to get you to come around."

"Could be," Dena said, "but I was in the sixth grade."

Rodney concluded a very long interview by telling us, "Most people that meet us go away saying, 'How could they possibly be happy knowing what they know?' [Rodney was dying at the age of fifty-two from a neurological disorder similar to ALS.] But my happiness is waking up with her every morning and being with her as much as possible. And you know, work is important, it truly is, and I believe in hard work. I've always been a hard worker. But I never understood until now how happy one person can make you. And although I've always been happy with Dena, I never knew before now how truly happy I am."

In discussing his marriage, William S. sounded a bit like Rodney in his overuse of the word *very*: "Well, it's been a very, very, very wonderful life. Very good. Super. I got the best mate in the world. . . . The smartest thing that I did was marrying her. She's been a real humdinger! And I don't mind if she knows it! In fact I'm quite glad that she knows it." His wife responded with similar exuberance: "Goody, goody, goody, okay!"

Mary T. boiled earthly joy down to two words: "Being loved."

Perhaps the best way to get a feel for what really matters to people who are reviewing their life is to pick a random point and just go down the list of the responses to this question of what brings the most joy. Listen to the amazing consistency of these answers; and remember, this list represents the responses of a wide spectrum of people.

- Rose D.—"My family—children, grandchildren, and great-grandchildren"

- Lois—"Grandchildren, who will answer the phone when I call"
- William S.—"Marrying her and my family"
- Chester—"My two kids turned out good"
- Mildred M.—"I'd say my kids"
- Mary T.—"My children, it made me think I'd done something right"
- Donald—"Family"
- Anna—"Daughter, family, everybody getting along"
- John H.—"The lady I'm married to"
- Christine—"The people close to me"
- James B.—"That I married Julia, thirty-three years of marriage, and two wonderful boys"
- Lena—"My three children"
- Sam—"Children turned out well and a wife that loved me"

At the risk of being redundant, here are a few more so you can get the real "feel" of what was said:

- Jerry—"My kids, you know, my son"
- Harold M.—"Marrying my wife; the day I got married my knees were shaking"
- Mildred—"My contribution to my church work and my husband and son are exceptional, [along with] the joy of being with my grandchildren"
- Reitha—"What can I leave? My legacy is my children. I'm most proud of being a mother and that my family is still together"
- Charles W.—"My family and friends; greatest joy is the day she asked me to marry her"

- James G.—"My family, my joy is having my family to-gether"
- James A.—"I'm proud of my life, I have a fine wife and a fine son and daughter and son-in-law and grandchildren"
- Gary—"The birth of my son and my relationship with Jesus Christ"
- Louise O.—"My three sons"
- David D.—"My boys, my two boys"
- Leon—"My friends" (Leon had no surviving family members)
- Lillie—"My family—my husband, child, and grand-daughter"
- Mickey—"Our children, having our children together"

The list goes on with amazingly consistent responses. Occasionally there are other responses such as "I'm extremely proud of my professional life," but as a workaholic myself, I was simply amazed at how rarely people's work life was even mentioned.

Being in a "life review" mode really seemed to bring some unique perspective and focus to people. As Thomas D. thought over what brought him the greatest joy he said, "My four children and my ex-wife and my wife." He included his ex-wife? Willie Q. said, "I've been married twice and I made it through both of them, I guess. I had a lot more than I thought in my first wife." Looking back they both see that things were better than they realized at the time. Their observations should give us, the healthy and thriving, pause to consider what really brings us joy today. What is it? Is it right there in front of us? Do we really even think consciously about creating joy in life? Or, do we just live life in some random pattern and find joy from time to time, but without really knowing how or why?

How much daily effort are we actually directing toward creating joy in our lives? Several years ago a psychologist friend of ours spoke, in very general terms, of a conversation he had with an unhappy client. He asked this woman in her forties to tell him of an activity that brought her peace and joy. Her eyes lit up immediately as she told him, "I just love to go fishing. There's something about being around the water and out in nature that just renews me and gives me great joy." He then asked her when she had last gone fishing. She thought for a few seconds and said, "I guess it's been about fifteen years." No wonder she was unhappy! I'm not even a trained psychologist, but I can tell her how to "get happy"—GO FISHING, for goodness' sake. Start doing things that make you happy. So often we let our jobs, our volunteer commitments, and even our friends and family dictate to us what we should do and how we should feel.

One of many amazing findings in our interviews was the fact that the things that brought joy to people were so readily available. The "quest" for joy doesn't require you make a long journey or save your money; we're surrounded by joy. To repeat Christine, "There's just such joy all around." When we talked to the soon-departed, they almost all seemed to realize joy was within reach—and, more important, it had been all along.

"Time Is on My Side"

The Rolling Stones sang, "Time is on my side."[3] Yes it is, but sometimes it doesn't seem that way. We often say we just don't have time to do the most important things that bring the greatest joy to our lives. We complain that we just don't have enough time to get everything done today. Yet, in reality we all have the same amount of time in a day. And we all have all the time there is.

Money is the biggest discriminator in society. It separates people according to what they are able to acquire, control, and spend. Time, however, is the most powerful equalizer. As we thought about time and life we came to the realization that, while dollars are the currency of the U.S. economy, time is the currency of life. Seconds, minutes, hours, days, and years are the denominations of this currency. We all have 3,600 seconds per hour, 86,400 seconds per day, and a whopping 31,536,000 seconds per year (except for leap years when we get a bonus 86,400 seconds). These are huge numbers. If you really think about it, time is actually abundant. And at the end of the day, financially rich people don't have any more than those considered poor. What none of us know and what will always remain one of the great mysteries of life, is how much time we have in the future. With the exception of the day on which you die, you do know how much time you have for each day.

One critical difference between the nature of the currency of our economy/money, and the currency of life/time, is that money can be saved and accumulated for use in the future. Time cannot. Speculation about what we would do if we "could put time in a bottle" makes for a great Jim Croce song, but we can't put time in a bottle. At the end of every day, we have, in the currency of life, "spent" all 86,400 seconds we received for that day. Every single second is gone, used up, and vanished, and we cannot have it back. While we say money has to be earned, time is a gift, and that is further evidence that life is a gift!

Chapter 2

GATHERING AROUND

According to popular wisdom, "You can't take it with you." But time and time again we saw people gathering up their treasure at the end of life, clutching more tightly to their riches as death approached. Don't misunderstand: there were no money-grubbers among the 104 hospice patients we interviewed. Few of them seemed to care about material possessions one way or another. But their true wealth—the relationships that brought genuine richness to their lives—they jealously guarded and clutched with white-knuckled determination.

Did they think they could take it with them? In a way, I suspect they did. Facing eternity, they turned their attention toward one of the few things on earth stronger than death—namely, love.

One of the most obvious patterns we observed, both in our interviews and in the actual experience of the visits themselves, was the gathering of people around those who were dying. It is such a common pattern of behavior we probably take it for granted. It isn't always possible for people to actually be there in person, but it is clear most people want to spend quality time with people they love as they approach death. The same pattern can be observed at funerals and memorial services. People gather around at those times to honor the life of the departed as well as to provide support and encouragement for the closest family and friends in their grief. But it was clear from our conversations that the soon-departed would much prefer that people come and gather around while they were still alive. Some even took extraordinary measures to assure they would be able to spend quality time with their loved ones in those last days on earth.

The beautiful love story of Julia and Larry is told later in this book. But Julia was loved by many more people than just her husband, and those people began gathering around toward the end of her life. Larry told us Julia "has gotten hundreds and hundreds, probably five or six hundred cards and letters from people that tell how she's had an impact on their lives. How else would you ever hear that?"

Julia spent thirty years teaching five-year-olds. Larry said,

The day we got the diagnosis we were in the depths of depression, and we walked in the door and the mail was there. There was an envelope in that group from a young boy who's now the minister of college-age young people at First Baptist Dallas, the biggest Baptist church in the country. He was telling her how important it was what she taught him as a five-year-old and how it ultimately led to his full-time vocation. I mean, that's affirming, and that's what a lot of these letters are, just affirming what

[she] meant to [them] and how [she] impacted [them] and how [she] made [them] feel.

Larry went on to paraphrase Maya Angelou: "People may forget what you say, but they never forget how you make them feel." In Julia's life the tables were now turned, and the hundreds of well-wishers were making her feel loved and proud of her life.

Julia was unable to speak at the time of our interview, but she did use a computer system to spell out some basic ideas that allowed Larry to elaborate on her behalf. "The prayers of the people are being rained down on us. We receive the blessings. That's the beauty of it. I've never experienced anything like this, when you're held up [in prayer] by so many hundreds of people."

Consider Beverly's story, another example of a dying woman who refused to let life just happen to her, but was intentional about making sure she took care of some things before she died. You've seen all those ads for financial services companies in which they encourage people to start thinking about the legacy they'll leave for their children and grandchildren. That's exactly what Beverly did. When she realized she was dying, she got serious about what she was going to leave her family. She talked to her stockbroker, just like those "prepare for the future" ads say you're supposed to. But the conversation didn't follow the implied script.

Beverly wasn't calling for estate-planning purposes. She was calling to cash out. She sold enough stock to pay for a week at a huge house on the beach so she could be together with the whole family—seventeen people in all—one last time. She "raided" the account that was supposed to be her children's inheritance. She understood that there was a lot more to her legacy than a stock portfolio.

Beverly and her husband renewed their wedding vows that week in a spontaneous beach ceremony planned and executed in about fifteen hours ("It was a lot more beautiful than the last time," she remarked). She had tea parties with her granddaughters; her grandsons were so jealous of their time together that she had to give them a "gentlemen's coffee party" the next day. The family shot four hours of video of the children and grandchildren telling their favorite memories of Beverly. The kids wrote songs about her and performed them at night.

It was the first time the whole family had been together for an entire week, but it was such a special time they committed to begin getting together annually. That's truly a legacy, the result of intentionality.

Intentionality—that may be the biggest difference between people who know they're dying and people for whom it is still possible to avoid facing their own mortality. Beverly wasn't just skating through, and neither were any of the other people we interviewed for this book. "When the cancer came back the second time," she said, "I started living my life like I knew we were supposed to give our life to God. I started doing the things that I should do. I just have so many people that I have loved, and they've loved me back. . . . I've enjoyed every day that I've chosen to do this."

Time and time again our discussions focused on people "gathering around" to share those last moments together. Florence told us how thoughts, prayers, and cards really do make a difference, even if you can't be there in person.

When I get blue, and I do, and those times I ask why, those times linger on a long time. They feel long, but I don't know what is ahead of me the next day. I stop and try to think of the good things, things that I've been blessed with and the people that I met and have crossed paths with. I didn't realize until something like this comes up, that even though you're not there, you're thought of in prayers and cards. I've gotten lots and lots of cards and telephone calls and things from my friends. You can't imagine what that does to me. It makes me feel very humble and blessed.

To know people are praying for you, and to even know it when they are not present, demonstrates a spiritual sensitivity that seems to be enhanced by the nearness of death.

In addition to family members, so many of the people we talked with pointed to people in their church as the ones who gathered around them. Mildred told us her Sunday school class brought dinner every other night for the first two months after her diagnosis. "That gives me much joy. . . . And there has not been over five days when I haven't received a card from somebody, and sometimes it's been ten or twelve." Maver had a very similar experience. "My Christian friends at church . . . have really stood by me and they really do check on me. They visit me a lot. I get cards. I get so many cards. It takes me a long time to open them up."

Harriet was strengthened by prayer:

[I've had] lots and lots of prayers. I'm on my hairdress-er's prayer list and she tells people about me, and I'm on their prayer list. I don't even know how many of them there are. So I'm sure that's what kept me going this year, and my faith. . . . I had an imaginary sign over my door that says, "You can't leave here without praying." [When people came to visit] everybody knew that real quick. So it's still there but now we pray and say, "Thank You that I'm still here." People couldn't leave without praying. I've had lots of support from my church, lots of support from my family. One Sunday afternoon I had forty-five visitors at the hospital. They had to stop them at the elevator. I had people that day that came from Chicago, from Columbia, South Carolina, and we couldn't even get those people in the room that had driven all day in the snow in January to come to visit me. . . . So everybody was there, seeing me for the last time. It was just a real life-changing experience for me.

Even though Harriet was dying, I don't doubt her thankfulness was genuine. The gathering around was a life-changing experience. Do we have to reach the point of death to gain the insights Harriet did—to realize so many people genuinely care? For that matter, it doesn't even have to be that "so many" people genuinely care for us; it could simply be the revelation that *someone* genuinely cares for us. Is it possible to begin to deeply understand this at an early age?

William S. was a pastor. His wife reports:

An awful lot of people have come to visit us since he got sick. A couple of ladies from the congregation in Florida came up and a couple of men from the [same] congregation, and a lot of relatives. His brother has come to see us twice and they hadn't seen each other for years. And nieces and nephews and friends from seminary. There was a friend that came two weeks ago and he and his wife had been in seminary with us. . . . There was another couple who came . . . gosh, we've known these people for fifty or sixty years and they're still coming back!

It's not unusual for today's church to be criticized for being divisive, political, self-serving, and frankly, just plain mean at times. Some churches are giving "religion" a bad name. Those are tough words, especially in describing an institution Jesus loved. Could it be the "church people" in these stories, who demonstrated such love and compassion and Jesus-like behavior, were practicing a form of what James describes as "pure religion": "This is pure and undefiled religion in the sight of our God and Father, to visit orphans and widows in their distress . . . " (James 1:27).

In Matthew 25, Jesus describes the judgment and how some will be invited into the kingdom because of how they treated the king when he was hungry, thirsty, a stranger, naked, sick, and in prison. And the righteous ask the king, "When did we see you [this way?]" (v. 37). The king's response describes the essence of Christian behavior: "to the extent that you did it to one of these brothers of Mine, even the least of them, you did it to Me" (v. 40). Jesus said, "I was sick and you visited Me"—this is "pure and undefiled religion" in the sight of God. . . . For the church to shine in today's society, it needs to get back to the basics.

I've always been moved by the song "The Living Years" by Mike and the Mechanics.

I wasn't there that morning,
When my Father passed away.
I didn't get to tell him
All the things I had to say …
I just wish I could have told him
In the living years.[1]

This song laments the failure of a father and son to reconcile before the father's death. The issues between the two that did not get addressed "in the living years" have now turned into regrets. A common saying in the business world is that 90 percent of success in life comes from simply showing up. There is no better application of this saying than in the process of reconciliation. The first and probably most difficult step in reconciliation is simply showing up.

I actually was there that morning when my father passed away. I did get to tell him all the things I had to say. That experience, as difficult and sad as it was, is one I treasure. It is probably impossible to explain why it meant so much to be there, but it did. Perhaps some of it had to do with conversations leading up to that day, conversations that went well beyond the routine exchanges between a father and son. Conversations that provide a sort of "safety check" that all important issues were reconciled. But it's much more than that. We were all there—my mother, my two sisters, my wife, and others. In the core of my being, it was simply a deeply felt moment that endures.

When we learn that a person we love is sick or dying, it is not uncommon to feel helpless and lament that there's nothing we can do. These stories make it clear that there are at least two things anyone can do for someone in these circumstances. First, anyone can pray. And it is clear that in every one of these cases the soon-departed actually felt the prayers of others, so no one can say prayer doesn't matter. The second thing anyone can do is show up. Communicate your love and care in a card, a phone call, an e-mail, a text message, a letter, or, if possible, in person. These people have taught us to never again underestimate the value of this human connection we call communication.

All these stories raise the question "Why do we gather around?" The answer is probably more intuitive than it is rational: people need people. We sense that it will be our turn someday to face death. We know death is a pretty scary thing to most people, especially until they come to terms. We know gathering encourages people, and another way to write the word is EnCourage—to give courage that overcomes fear.

You can't take it with you—not material riches, anyway. Earthly treasures rust and become corrupt. Material goods are all left behind. Maybe gathering people around us as we prepare to depart this world has something to do with our desire to take our treasures with us, and now we see clearly that our only lasting treasures are the people who surround us. And, in the end, we can take them with us.

Some Go On Ahead and Some Are Left Behind

Death is often more difficult for those left behind than it is for those who go on ahead. It certainly seemed that way when one of our close relatives went on ahead at the age of sixteen. David had been diagnosed with muscular dystrophy at the age of four. His parents totally changed their lives to be able to care for David and to seek every possible opportunity for David to get better. They took frequent trips, moved into a house specifically designed for David, changed work patterns to have time to care for David. Their devotion to their son is the greatest demonstration of love we have ever encountered.

At the memorial service some of David's favorite memories were on display—pictures with his parents, pictures with friends and relatives and his dog Frazier, Arkansas Razorback memorabilia, autographs from Vince Gill (David referred to Vince Gill simply as "the man") and Amy Grant. The service was a wonderful reminder of the precious life David lived. We were making it through the service okay until we came to the final item on the program. As we sat remembering David, the unmistakably sweet voice of Vince Gill filled the room as "Go Rest High on That Mountain"[2] emanated from the sound system.

What a great picture of the transition from life to life. It's not that they are gone; they've just gone on ahead. Vince Gill wrote this song for himself when his brother died as a young man. Through his music, he prepared David to see that he would simply go ahead and wait, "high on that mountain." He also reminded all of us left behind that a day would come when we will be reunited with the people we love who have gone ahead.

Chapter 3

LIVING THE MOMENT

Strange as it sounds, most of "the 104" were grateful for the fact they were dying slowly rather than suddenly and unexpectedly. Their terminal condition gave them the opportunity to tie up loose ends, to say the things they needed to say. It also gave their loved ones the opportunity to close accounts.

Perhaps the biggest blessing enjoyed by hospice patients is the fact they are set free from the need to continually look to the future. Life, they realize, is what is happening in the present, and they seize the day with all the energies they can muster. Larry, for instance, talked about a decision he and his wife, Julia, made immediately after she received her terminal diagnosis: "We made a determination when we came home that we were going to live our lives as fully and completely as possible."

Most of our interviewees were living fully in the moment for the first time in their lives. It was such a transformative thing for them that everybody seemed to be talking about living in the moment, seizing the day:

- "Live! Live! Don't say 'I'll do it tomorrow.' Do it today 'cause you'll be sorry when tomorrow comes."—Lois
- "Live every day to the fullest, because God never promised tomorrow!"—Linda
- "Well, I think you have to take every day one at a time."—George
- "Live life every day, to enjoy every day because to-morrow is not promised to anybody. Enjoy every day."—David D.
- "Live every day, and enjoy every day because it may be your last. And live your life, don't let the disease live it for you."—Rodney
- "Live one day at a time and pray like it's the last one."—Julia O.
- "I would tell people to enjoy each day and stop get-ting caught up in [the future]. You don't know what is left."—Christine
- "Live life to the fullest, and don't look back over your shoulder to see who's chasing you. Live it day by day. Any problems that come up, solve them at that time. If you make mistakes, no regrets!"—Laurence
- "Live it! Don't feel sorry for yourself . . . you'll never get out of this life alive. . . . That's about the whole thing right there!"—Chester
- "Just do your best. Do your best. . . . Just take one day at a time. . . . It might be the last. Just take one day at a time. You take it as it comes."—Mickey
- "Live life to the fullest, as best you can, and hope and

pray for the best. . . . That's about all any of us can do."—Jane

Those look like clichés, especially lined up like that, with no context. I understand that. But trust me: those words had a very different effect coming from people who fully felt the truth of the statement "Tomorrow is not promised to anybody." Those of us who are situated squarely in the land of the living are inoculated against the wonder, excitement, and urgency that come with really believing you're going to die. For the soon-departed, wonder, excitement, and urgency have broken through to them.

Carmen related something a friend told her that made a big difference in her life:

When you're driving to work and you're thinking about what you left at home, you're looking in the past. And if you're thinking about what you're going to do at work, you're looking into the future. Meanwhile, *you're dead!* I thought, *You know, that makes a whole lot of sense.* I started looking around when I was driving to work and I saw old buildings that I didn't even know were there . . . Pay attention to where you're at.

That does make a lot of sense. Two places where we can't live are in the past and in the future; we're dead there. The only place we can actually live is in the present. Maybe that's why so many people seem to stumble along—they're dead!

Charles Dickens addressed the same phenomenon in his classic *A Christmas Carol.* Ebenezer Scrooge is given the opportunity not only to review his current life, but to look into the past and the future. As the Ghosts of Christmas Past, Christmas Present, and Christmas Future make their visits, Scrooge grows increasingly horrified to realize he doesn't really know what matters in life. In the finale of the story, Scrooge understands that this terrifying experience is in fact the greatest blessing of his life. He comes to realize he still has time to redeem his life. He also learns that the only time he can take redemptive action is in the present. If this fictional experience could be created in each of us, what would we see? Would we, like Scrooge, be horrified, or would we be confident that we are living our life in the knowledge and corresponding action of what really matters?

The words of Harold G. reflect the same admonition for us to live in the present:

Look to this day, for it is life, the very life of life, for yesterday is but a dream and tomorrow is but a vision, but today we will live. So that's an old proverb that sums it up in [a] beautiful, poetic way. But to live in the now is the greatest thing I could tell anybody as to how to live life. If I live in the past, I'm going to live in regrets, I'm going to live in guilt. I'm going to live in shame. I'm going to live in all the fears, all the negatives that you can think of; if I live in the past, I'm going to live that way. I don't want those feelings. If I live in the future, I'm going to have all kinds of disappointments. I'm going to project and say, "Tomorrow I'm going to do this or I'm going to do that" . . . and something happens tomorrow and I can't do this . . . and we're disappointed. People live in disappointment because they primarily live in the future.

What an insight! Living in the future is the double whammy: it robs us of joy when we miss out on the present, and it keeps us from enjoying the future when it gets here, since the future inevitably doesn't match up with the future we've concocted in our heads. One of the rarely mentioned joys of living in the present is that it leaves us open to the surprises and mysteries of the future.

Harold went on to say,

There's another story of an old fellow that says when he was growing up, when he was four or five years old he thought, *Oh boy, won't it be great when I get to be in school! Everything will be just wonderful, when I go to school, when I get to go to school!* So the time comes and he goes to school and then as time goes on he thinks, *Won't it be wonderful when I get out of grade school and I can be in high school!* So the time comes and he goes to high school and thinks, *Won't it be wonderful when I can graduate from high school and I'll be somebody, and I'll get a job. I can go to college!* Then he goes to college and he gets a job and thinks, *Oh, won't it be wonderful whenever I can, oh, there's a beautiful lady* and they get married. Then he thinks, *Won't it be wonderful when the first child comes along* and the first child comes along. *Won't it be wonderful when the next one and the next one comes along* and then all the children are there. And then he thinks, *Won't it be wonderful to be able to do for these children what I wasn't able to do for myself* and all this happens and then the time for retirement comes. *Won't it be wonderful when I can retire!* And, so in preparation for retirement, they build a beautiful little retirement home out on the lake and it's got a beautiful front porch and it's got the rocking chairs on the front porch and the day of retirement comes and the company gives him the watch, and he goes and draws his social security, and he sits on the front porch, he and his wife. And what do they do? They talk about the good old days!

That's how life is lived. Always in the future. If we could just live today, live in the now, it would be so wonderful. I mean, it's an experience that nobody could imagine how good it is. It doesn't mean that you can't make plans. One of my counselors put it the best I've ever heard—she said, "It's okay to plan—just don't pack because you might be disappointed." Life is full of disappointments, but those disappointments only come if we've already packed!

There it is: make plans, just don't pack your bags too early. Even though we're not guaranteed tomorrow, we still have to plan for it. We still have to buy insurance, patch the roof, learn skills that will be useful in the future. The question is, how much of your heart is set on the future to the exclusion of the present? If you have your bags packed and are sitting on the curb waiting for the bus, you aren't living life to the fullest!

Charles D. said,

Enjoy every moment of it 'cause you never know when it's going to end. . . . I'd been wanting to go elk hunting for years and years. . . . We kept putting it off, putting it off, putting it off, and Elmer told me, "You need to go, 'cause you never know—you keep putting it off, you're gonna run outta days."

His wife said,

Him and his brother had been trying to go elk hunting forever and it was always either he had to work or none of them had the money . . . it was always something. And this last year I told him, "You're going elk hunting, whether anybody else can go or not. I'm making reservations for you; I'm putting it on the card, you're going elk hunting." Well, his brother just happened to get time off and was able to go with him . . . they had a great time!

Because of the brain tumor, sixteen-year-old Thomas H. could barely hear. His mother was able to speak very loudly to get him to hear some of our questions. We asked her to tell us what would be the combined answer for her and Thomas regarding our message for the world? "Life is too short," she said. "What you do with your life is a choice, you have to choose how to live, and it's not always easy. It may not be a happy day. But you have to live every minute of every day for that minute. And, you have to choose to enjoy every minute of every day."

Even in these incredibly difficult situations, we were meeting and talking with people who were choosing to live in the moment and who were choosing to enjoy that minute. These conversations have helped us understand that living in the moment is really an attitude—a predisposition to respond to events with a certain pattern of thinking or behavior. Thomas's mother was describing a powerful attitude: no matter whether it was a good day or bad day, they chose to enjoy life.

Christine said happiness for her was very simple:

Watching the sunset on my swing. Watching the hummingbirds, watching the other birds, watching the squirrels, and watching these crazy cats and some (of) the things they go through. They love the dog. The dog loves [them]. She (the dog) gives them a bath and they (the cats) clean her ears, little things like that. There's so much joy all around but it's a shame that it takes something like this, when you've been so busy, to open your eyes and see it. I would strongly advise everyone to take at least one day a month like Jesus says and just go away, come away to a quiet place by yourself. He went on vacation. He met alone with God. He didn't have time for eating or sleeping because there were so many people hassling Him, there were so many things to do. Take a little time, a little quiet spot where you can go. Whatever your beliefs are in God, just take them to Him, be still and listen and enjoy what's around you. It's pretty simple. I don't have profound words.

Not profound? No, Christine was very profound—especially if you choose to put her words into action.

As Christine's words show, living in the present is often a matter of taking advantage of life's simplest pleasures. Charles D. talked about the pleasure of sitting on his back porch watching the fish pond, seeing the deer come out of the woods to drink, watching the wild turkeys strut across his yard. Those kinds of pleasures require that you live in the moment.

I love what Kathleen said on this point:

> The greatest joy in my life is getting up at three o'clock in the morning, and I can't sleep and I come in and I sit down, and I sit here in my chair and I rock and there is one bird that comes and sits outside in the tree and sings in the quiet of the night, and sings this beautiful song, and I get so much pleasure out of that song.

I've often thought about Kathleen sitting in her rocker in the wee hours of the morning, and that night bird singing comfort and joy into her soul. And I wonder how that routine got started. When most of us can't sleep at three in the morning, we shut our eyes tighter, wrap the pillow around our ears to get as much quiet as possible, try to will ourselves to sleep. *I've got to get up in the morning. Tomorrow's going to be a disaster if I don't get some sleep. What's going to become of me if I'm not fresh and ready for my ten o'clock presentation?* But Kathleen got out of bed and sat in her rocking chair to see what joy the world might bring her. And she met a little bird that became one of the chief joys of her life. The soon-departed understand that even three in the morning is "the present"—a place to live.

Maybe the best context was provided by James B. when we asked him to provide his message to the world. He answered, "Live your dash!" Not understanding, we asked him to repeat himself. "Live your dash," he said again. "You know—you were born in 1946, dash, lived till 2000."

We asked this former business executive to explain how a person could "live their dash." His response was classic. "So many people just, you know, they get up, they're not really in life, they don't really enjoy the job they have, they putter around. . . . They don't care. They're just out there but they're wandering lost. They really need to get off of it and try to do something."

If you let them, the lessons shared by these soon-departed will confront you with what is really important in life. Rather than thinking, *I know someone who needs to hear these stories and be challenged to change*, why not start with the man or woman in the mirror? You may think you agree with James and know someone who is "just out there . . . wandering lost." But the real challenge is to look inside yourself for that portion of your own being that is "wandering lost," and give yourself direction.

Don't Worry . . .

In 1989 a cute novelty song by Bobby McFerrin won the Grammy for Song of the Year. "Don't Worry, Be Happy" was a smash hit, becoming the first a cappella song to reach number one on the Billboard pop charts. The simplicity of the message is a huge part of its appeal.

In every life there comes some trouble
When you worry you make it double.
Don't Worry. Be Happy![1]

Simple, but very true. Worry is one of the most peculiar of human habits. It never helps anything, it often makes things worse,

*and the great majority of things we worry about never come
to pass. What if we all took Bobby McFerrin at his word and
stopped worrying? I don't have any scientific data to cite, but I
can just remember people being a little happier when that song
was at the peak of its popularity. A psychologist friend of mine
told me his business dropped off during that time. He joked that
he even considered disconnecting the piped-in music in his waiting room. He was concerned his clients would hear that song
and then just get up and leave!*

Death Speaks

*The certainty of death rang out clearly from the words of Wil-
liam M. "I came into this world to die. No question about it. It's
fundamental, everyone has to die and pass judgment. That's two
appointments that you're not gonna be late for and you're not
gonna miss."*

In his play Sheppey, *W. Somerset Maugham retold an old story
about a man who tried to miss his own appointment with death.
This story is quoted as a prologue to John O'Hara's novel* Appointment in Samarra, *which takes its name from the story.*

> *There was a merchant in Baghdad who sent his ser-
vant to market to buy provisions and in a little while the
servant came back, white and trembling, and said, Master,
just now when I was in the market-place I was jostled by
a woman in the crowd and when I turned I saw it was
Death that jostled me. She looked at me and made a*

threatening gesture; now, lend me your horse, and I will ride away from the this city and avoid my fate. I will go to Samarra and there Death will not find me. The merchant lent him his horse, and the servant mounted it, and he dug his spurs in its flanks and as fast as the horse could gallop he went. Then the merchant went down to the market-place and he saw me standing in the crowd and he came to me and said, "Why did you make a threatening gesture to my servant when you saw him this morning?" That was not a threatening gesture, I said, it was only a start of surprise. I was astonished to see him in Baghdad, for I had an appointment with him tonight in Samarra.[2]

Chapter 4

A COLORING BOOK–
MADDIE'S STORY

How do you ask a five-year-old to tell you about her life and to answer such questions as: *What has brought you the greatest joy in life? What do you regret? What is the most important thing you've ever done?* or *If you could give a message to the whole world about how to live life, what would it be?* Does a five-year-old have anything profound to tell us? Does she know what really matters?

Interviewing Maddie was different from any of the other interviews we did. Although only five years old, she was suffering from a rare neurological disorder characterized by the development of small tumors on nerve endings. As you might imagine, the physical pain was excruciating. Her physicians and the staff at Alive Hospice did much to help to manage the pain, but it was still tough on Maddie and her family. The courage and strength of spirit we saw in this little girl sets a high standard for us all.

Maddie's mother, Jennifer, said the diagnosis developed gradually. Maddie was a "cranky baby" with low muscle tone. At nine months she wasn't hitting her developmental milestones, and they realized they had a child with developmental delays. That in itself was a big deal to Maddie's parents. But things soon got worse.

Not much later, major swelling started to develop on Maddie's face. On her parents' fifth wedding anniversary, Maddie was admitted to Vanderbilt Children's Hospital with a preliminary diagnosis of cancer. A couple of days later, the doctors realized Maddie didn't have cancer, but neurofibromentosis. "All we could feel was enormous relief because we thought, *She doesn't have cancer*," Jennifer said. But that relief soon gave way to sorrow as Maddie's parents realized what their precious daughter was in for. "It turned out, with cancer I think you either know if you have resolution, you either kick it or you don't. With this it just progresses and progresses and can be a very torturous disease. It's very painful for her and it's been a roller coaster because you never know what's going to happen."

And yet Maddie, when we spoke to her, was the most delightful little five-year-old you could hope to meet. She was bright and cheerful, interested in all the things you would expect a five-year-old girl to be interested in. She loved Disney. She loved to paint (purple was her favorite color). She loved cake, especially chocolate and strawberry. The striking thing was how much she loved her life. "Maddie is really zealous," her mother said. "She is my joy. Such mundane things that other children can pass by and ignore . . ." She broke off crying, unable to finish her sentence. Maddie's courage in the face of constant pain was truly an inspiration.

We asked Maddie a question that we didn't ask any of our other interviewees: "If there was a book called *Maddie's Life*, what kind of book would it be?" Her answer dispelled any doubts about whether or not we would have anything to learn from a five-year-old.

"It would be a coloring book," she said. She then began to paint a verbal picture of a beautiful girl and her wonderful family. She would color green grass and yellow flowers in her coloring book—planting flowers and tending the garden, after all, were among her favorite things to do.

We asked Maddie to turn her coloring book to a page that showed her when she was happiest. She described this page as one that would show Maddie sitting in her mother's lap. Her dad would be there. Her cat Tomasina would be in her lap, and her brother/protector Palmer would be there, too, but, she stipulated, "He wouldn't be touching me!"

Of all our interviewees, perhaps Maddie was the most in touch with the simplest pleasures life offers. I asked her what made her really happy. "When the sun's out there," she answered. An amazing answer! It's so easy to let life's pressures make us forget such simple blessings as the sunshine—but Maddie didn't forget.

Every morning Maddie picked out her father's tie for work. What a beautiful little ritual of domestic intimacy, the little girl taking care of the man who took care of her. "She loves to pick Daddy's ties out every morning," her mother observed.

I asked, "What colors do you pick for him? Red?"

"No, pink!" Maddie said. But she was only teasing. Maddie's mother pointed out that her husband didn't own a pink tie. "She has a very ornery sense of humor," her mother told me. "She's very spunky. At times her humor is almost bordering inappropriate." But she thought about what she said and backed up: for a girl in Maddie's situation, what could be inappropriate?

Maddie's zeal was incredible, and it manifested itself in so many ways. Her mother told about the time she rode the roller coasters at Walt Disney World:

> Everybody was screaming, and Maddie was grinning. We were treating her as fragile, as if she didn't need to go on those types of rides. She got very upset. She's very tall for her age, so when she met the height criteria, she rode them. They took snapshots, and Maddie was the only one who wasn't screaming coming down the thing. She was just sitting there smiling like, "This is great!"

If Maddie was wide open on the roller coaster, she was just as wide open with her love. "She's an overly affectionate child," her mother said. "You don't usually meet kids that are this unselfish with their love. She's very grateful and loving, and all day long she tells you she loves you and is affectionate and hugging and kissing." I experienced it myself. Though we had just met, she gave me a good-bye hug and kiss on the cheek when we parted ways. And I was moved to hear her tell her mother, "I love you more than stars."

"It brings joy into a room when she comes," Maddie's mother said. That's quite a legacy for a five-year old.

An equally important legacy was the admonition to live in the present and to be grateful for the simple pleasures. Her mother said,

> This morning when she woke up and she was perky and herself, you just want to leap and jump through the hall-

ways because you just think, you know, you got one more good day. You have another one. You enjoy the little things in life, you don't sweat the big things. You learn what a real problem is. You're not as petty. . . . If she wants to wear Halloween costumes at inappropriate times, and makeup or glitter, you do it, because you want to live in the moment. She's taught us to live in the moment.

Maddie's mother grew up the child of ministers, but it was her experience with her daughter that really taught her what God was like. Of the time before she and her husband had a sick child, she said, "We thought we were this young healthy couple, Christians, we felt that we had this blanket of protection from anything bad ever happening to us." But they found out God had something else in mind for them—something better, though it didn't seem so at first.

I became very confused at first because I couldn't understand how a God that's so merciful and compassionate could allow something like this to happen. But now I can certainly see that the plan was way beyond that. It taught me that God is in control. I can't be angry at Him just because something bad happened to us. . . . I think that it taught us about grace. She taught me what grace really is.

That's an amazing thing for a mother to say. Suffering through a child's terminal—and excruciatingly painful—illness is a kind of grace.

I think it's a plan of God's perfect grace in my child. I think it's only His grace that keeps me going. There's some days I haven't wanted to get out of bed because the idea of being with a child in pain . . . emotional things can be so overwhelming and you think, *I can't face this, I don't want to do this.* But you have to get up. You have to. I think the path the Lord has led me on in the last five years, it's taught me not to be complacent with anything. You don't take it for granted. You don't take for granted one good day, you don't take for granted the fact that she woke up today. Instead of me dwelling on a negative, it's easier to say, "Oh, God, look. She's happy. She's awake and she's happy." I get to have that.

Maddie was absolutely fearless. She certainly didn't fear death. No doubt that was partly the result of the fact that she didn't really have a concept of death at her age, but in any case, her courage gave courage to those around her. Here's what her mother had to say about fear and courage:

She's not afraid of [death], and I would rather it be that way. I have fears. How fear and relief can intertwine so much to me is baffling, because I have fears that today it could happen but I'm also afraid of it lingering too long. . . . I would rather it be before she has a good grasp of it because she might be afraid or she might not want to when you have no hope to offer her. . . . It's a day that you live in such fear of but yet you know in some ways you're going to feel relieved and that used to make me feel so guilty. But you know, you've got a five-year-old that can't function each day without morphine and the heavy hitters.

The complexity of her mother's emotions were a contrast to the simplicity of Maddie's. As our interview neared its conclusion we asked Maddie, "If you could give a message to the whole wide world, that everyone would hear, what would that message be?" After some consideration Maddie said she would want the whole world to know "that I'm a kindergartner girl!"

She was only five years old, but Maddie had a huge impact on the people around her. Maddie knew, just as well as the 102-year-old we talked with, what matters in life. In the most innocent, naïve way, the purity of her responses suggests that we all probably knew how to live at some point in our lives. Our hope is you will challenge yourself to regain some of the simple elegance children have about living.

A few months after our interview, soon after she turned six, Maddie went on ahead of us to heaven. The visitation with her family after her departure was especially hard. It would have been impossible except for their strong faith. Especially with children, we want to ask God why. Maddie was just the sweetest, most gentle, precious little girl you can imagine, and now she is gone. One truth that struck us right between the eyes was that if it was time for Maddie to go, then surely we shouldn't be surprised when our time arrives. We should live our lives expecting and believing we are going to die.

Songs of Love, a non-profit foundation based in Forest Hills, New York, cooperates with songwriters and artists from across the country to produce one-of-a-kind songs for children who are sick or dying. Belmont University is a cooperating partner whose students have written, produced, and performed numerous songs for children. After we met Maddie for the first time, it became clear that Maddie needed her own song. In such a talent-rich environment as Belmont, it wasn't long before one of its very best students, Lucas Boto, was on board. With the permission of Maddie's family we gave Lucas a copy of the interview transcript and he went to work writing the words and music and then performing the song as it was recorded in the on-campus studio.

Conducting these interviews was a tremendous privilege, even though in some cases, like Maddie's, we struggled. One of the things we've learned about life is that the times we struggle the hardest are most often the ones that become precious over time. But there was one moment in our time with Maddie that was nothing but a privilege and blessing. It was when we were able to deliver Maddie's song to her.

Maddie had been able to go home from the Alive Hospice facility for a time, so Judy and I delivered the song to her home. It was mid-afternoon and Maddie, her brother Palmer, her mother Jennifer, and two of her grandparents were present. As the song began Maddie listened intently and was surprised to hear the name of her brother Palmer. When she heard the song describe "a girl that's five," she said, "I'm five, Mommy!" And finally when the line "She's just Maddie, She's just Maddie!" came, she cried out, "That's me, it's about me!" The song's writer and performer couldn't be present for the presentation because he had returned to his home for the long Christmas break, but he agreed with us that we shouldn't wait—time was of the essence. Our prayer is that somehow, God will show Lucas Boto the smile and joy that he brought to Maddie and her entire family. God bless him.

"Maddie"
Written and sung by Lucas Boto

Now here's a girl that
Loves mom and dad
Can crack a joke and make you laugh
Let's not forget though
Her bigger bro'
His name is Palmer and he's her
Her Protector

'Cause she is worth so much
I don't know how love works
It just does

If I could paint a picture of a girl that's five
It would fill the canvas and make you smile
She's just too much to contain
And I can't fully explain
She's just Maddie
She's just Maddie

Like any woman
She loves her chocolate
And bright yellow flowers
Could simply make her day
Then there's Aunt "Wena"
Maddie can't get enough of her
While Tomasina crawls up in her lap

A moment frozen in time
One that words just can't describe

If I could write a book about this girl that's five
It would fill the pages and make you smile
She's just too much to contain
And I can't fully explain

She picks dad's tie, takes care of mommy
What a day
Atta girl Maddie
Baby girl don't ever change

If I could dream a dream about this girl that's five
It would last forever and make you smile
She's just too much to contain
And I can't fully explain
She's just Maddie
She's just Maddie

Life Is a Gift

September 11, 2001, was a day of tragedy for all Americans. Our family experienced the tragedy in a deeply personal way. Adam White was a remarkable young man, less than a month away from his twenty-seventh birthday. He was a pioneer in the trading of environmental credits, and led that division of Cantor Fitzgerald's business from an office in the World Trade Center. Adam's work and play took him around the world from business deals in Europe to trekking to base camp at Mt. Everest. Everyone who knew Adam White knows that he was a living example of the admonition to live every day to its fullest. He never passed up an opportunity for an adventure, and he never passed up a chance to make life fun for the people around him.

Our daughter Kelly was especially drawn to this life. Kelly and Adam had been dating for eight years. At work they could look out their windows and see one another's office. They were both in their offices early on September 11, 2001. Kelly witnessed the explosion from the tower across the street and immediately began to dial Adam on her cell phone. She was never able to get through.

We drove to New York to be with Kelly on September 12, and were finally able to enter the city on the early morning of the thirteenth when the bridges were reopened. While we made trips to the armory and checked the hospital lists, we gradually began to lose hope. We attended a memorial service in Baltimore for Adam on Saturday and then later attended a memorial service in Atlanta. Our hearts were broken. This was the first time I really experienced what this phrase means. A broken heart doesn't just mean that it hurts. It also means your heart just doesn't work right—feelings and emotions are so confused that sometimes you don't feel anything at all.

As Thanksgiving approached that year, I remembered that in August, prior to the September attack, I had agreed to give a Thanksgiving message to a local chamber of commerce. As I began to think of what I might say, the question emerged, "Why do I have to provide a Thanksgiving message this year?" I really didn't want to do it—what was I supposed to be thankful for? My heart was still broken.

It was about this time a friend provided a copy of the remark-

able book Tracks of a Fellow Struggler—Living and Growing Through Grief *by John Claypool. This book describes Claypool's own personal loss and grief as he and his wife lost their young daughter after a difficult battle with leukemia. While there is no way to capture the full richness of this book without reading it in its entirety, the core message we took with us was "Life is a gift" and "Every gift should be received with gratitude."*[1]

Maybe it was time to stop asking why and instead to express gratitude and to begin saying, "Thank you!" Thank you for the time we had. Thank you for a most remarkable life that brought joy never to be erased. Thank you for the example of how to live a full life, even if in a short time.

As I continued to think about what to say to a gathering expecting a Thanksgiving message, I reflected on Thanksgivings from my past. When I was a child my parents would recite Psalm 100 from the Bible. As my sisters and I grew older, we memorized this psalm and would participate in the recitation. When each of us came to have our own children, we adopted this practice on several occasions:

Make a joyful noise unto the LORD, all ye lands.
Serve the LORD with gladness: come before his presence with singing,
Know ye that the LORD he is God: it is he that hath made us, and not we ourselves; we are his people, and the sheep of his pasture.
Enter into his gates with thanksgiving, and into his courts with praise: be thankful unto him, and bless his name.
For the LORD is good; his mercy is everlasting; and his truth endureth to all generations. (Psalm 100 KJV)

There it was! Right in the middle of this short psalm in verse three: "Know ye that the LORD he is God: it is he that hath made us, and not we ourselves; we are his people, and the sheep of his pasture." We don't belong to ourselves, so we don't get to call the shots! We didn't create ourselves. We have been created and gifted with life. Every piece of that life should be lived with thankfulness and gratitude. And however long a life lasts, when it is over, we should be thankful for the gift we received from that life.

The overwhelming message from the people we interviewed was a message of gratitude for life and for the time given. We didn't encounter a lot of self-pity and asking God why. Instead, we found people wanting to grasp the remainder of the gift given them and a desire to make the very most of it.

Chapter 5

FINDING PURPOSE

I have been an extremely mean and cruel person," Lee said. "I have made grown men cry and bawl and everything you could think of." He was a veteran of the first Gulf War, a helicopter pilot whose job it was to face death every day. In his characteristically dry way, he said, "I've crashed more helicopters than most people have flown in." But it's one thing to face death in a helicopter, where, despite the risks, you still expect to survive by your skill or wit or luck. Facing certain death in a hospice bed is another thing altogether. As Lee said, "Life just got real short real fast!" It changes you. It certainly changed Lee.

Lee was a resident in the hospice facility when we met him. He spent much of his day just talking to his neighbors, a sort of amateur counselor.

Everybody that comes in here, if they come through that door, within a week I will know everybody in their family. I will know everything about them. People are always wanting to talk . . . they come to me and talk to me for two or three hours. What can you tell them? I mean, I'm not trained in any of this. They just want to talk, so I talk to them.

Lee found a purpose. He didn't call it a purpose, though. He called it his "map." It's an interesting choice of words. It suggests he had been wandering his whole life, but he finally found his way. "God still gives me another day. I haven't yet figured out my whole map. What am I supposed to do at the end of my life? But He's given me another day to figure it out. Any day you can put your feet on the ground is a beautiful day."

Lee spoke more than once about how mean he used to be, but it was hard to imagine, considering his description of a typical day now:

The first thing I did this morning was get up, go see [a fellow hospice patient] for a few minutes on the way out. Then I saw the two girls and their mother who just lost their father, and I talked to them for a minute. And the other man who's losing his wife. I stopped to talk to him for a minute. . . . Those people needed a shoulder, so why not give them one? If I had gotten up and looked at the floor and put my feet back in the bed, those families would still be sitting there in the hall. Maybe somebody else would have helped them. But maybe not.

From where he sat, he could see drug dealers plying their trade. Having found focus in his own life, it hurt his heart to see such aimlessness. "I still get up in the morning. I drink nasty coffee, and I will probably do something with my day. And every night I see these kids are across the street selling crack and doing drugs, every day. It's just such a waste."

———

A couple of years ago I heard Rabbi Harold Kushner talk about his book *Living a Life That Matters*[1] in which he examines the life of Jacob. The book of Genesis chronicles Jacob's life from his birth, to his youth (when he stole Esau's birthright and deceived his father to steal his older brother's blessing as well), to his exile, to his marriages (when he himself became the victim of the deception of his father-in-law), to the apex of his life: the night he wrestled with an angel (see Gen. 32:22–32). Kushner contends that the night Jacob had the dream about the ladder and wrestled with the angel, he was actually wrestling with himself, coming to the point of learning the real meaning of life and deciding what kind of life he should be living. Throughout his life, Jacob's struggles to that point were with relationship issues that emerged because he tended to value riches and self-gratification over friendship, loyalty, and love of other people. The morning after the struggle Jacob was physically limping, obviously harmed. He clearly "lost" the fight; but he actually won. He became a new person—a transformation so significant God changed his name from Jacob to Israel!

Lee wrestled with the angel, and the angel took him down, pinned him to the ground. But Lee turned the tables. He held on tightly and said, "I won't let go. Not until you bless me. Not until you let me see what this is all about. Not until I know *why*." The suffering we witnessed while researching this book led a lot of people to ask why. That's not surprising. The amazing thing is how many of them got an answer—an answer much bigger than the question they thought they were asking. They didn't get an answer to: "Why am I suffering?" They got an answer to: "Why am I here in the first place?"

> *I keep six honest serving men.*
> *(They taught me all I knew.)*
> *Their names are What and Why and When*
> *and How and Where and Who.*
>   —Rudyard Kipling[2]

It seems most people do "wrestle with the angel" to some degree at some point in life, but they don't usually endure in the struggle to a clear conclusion. They come away hurt, injured, bruised, and sore, but it ends up being for naught because they bail out before the fight is finished. They ask: "*What* am I supposed to learn from this? *Where* do I need to be? *How* do I do what I'm supposed to do? *Whom* should I hold responsible?" But they don't press on to ask that ultimate question: *Why?* Who, what, where, when, and how are of limited value without *why*. Our ultimate responsibility is to answer that question.

Sometimes I call *Why?* the "Scotty Morris question." Scotty Morris was a deep-thinking three-year-old who lived next door to me when I was in graduate school at the University of Arkansas. He wasn't afraid to ask why. (Maybe he was an angel?) If, for example, I was changing a flat tire, Scotty would walk up, survey the situation, and then ask, "What you doin'?"

"I'm changing a flat tire on my car."

"Why?"

"Because it won't roll."

"Why?"

"Because it's flat."

"Why?"

"Because it doesn't have any air pressure in it" (a touch of annoyance appearing in my voice).

"Why?"

"Because there's a hole in the tire" (clear exasperation now showing).

"Why?"

"Because someone must have been careless and dropped a nail in the road and I ran over it."

"Oh."

Whenever Scotty said, "Oh," I knew I had finally answered the question he was asking. We had reached the logical end of the line, and what I was doing now made sense to Scotty. He held on as tenaciously as Jacob himself.

Before we can answer the question "Why are we here—what is our purpose in life?" we must struggle through a process infinitely more tedious, painful, and frustrating than Scotty Morris could ever be. We must ask ourselves, "Why am I here?" and endure until we have an answer. Then we must ask the same question repeatedly, until we can no longer come up with a more fundamental answer. What seems to happen to a lot of people is they begin to struggle with *why* and they get frustrated, or get hurt, or become impatient, or just get tired and move on. The angel pins them, and they let go, sorry to be defeated but glad the struggle is over. And they haven't really learned anything. They can tell you with great confidence *what* and *where* and *how* and *when* and *who*, but they still can't tell you *why*.

"Is That All There Is?"

Peggy Lee became one of the most famous vocal performers of the twentieth century with scores of Top 40 jazz/pop hits. Tony Bennett referred to her as "the female Frank Sinatra." In 1969 she released what was probably her most remembered, or at least most discussed, recording, which soared to the top of the charts. "Is That All There Is?" struck a chord, and a mostly dissonant chord, with millions of people all over the world.

    The lyrics of the song express a sense of emptiness in life at the loss of a home in a fire, the sense that there was something missing, and the hollow feeling of love lost. In the final verse she sings that she's in no hurry for "that final disappointment . . . when that final moment comes and I'm breathing my last breath, I'll be saying to myself, is that all there is? Is that all there is? If that's all there is, my friends, then let's keep dancing, let's break out the booze and have a ball, if that's all there is."[3]

    The rationale here is not far removed from one life philosophy presented in Ecclesiastes—the eat, drink, and be merry approach. But we have to remember that approach was ultimately deemed to be "vanity," or a waste, by the author. "Is That All There Is?" is a troubling, somewhat depressing song and leaves that lingering question people have grappled with throughout human existence. On January 21, 2002, Peggy Lee died. She now knows for sure whether "that's all there is."

One of the questions we asked our interviewees was: "What is the most important thing you've ever done?" Five or six said, "I may not have done it yet." That's an amazing thing to think about. Every one of those people knew that they weren't going to live many more weeks. Yet they grasped the truth that there was good work left for them to do. As Lee (the chopper pilot) put it, "Every day there is something to do. Every day there is something you should do." For so many of our interviewees, their terminal diagnosis was like a new lease on life, a chance to focus on what really matters. It's ironic, but we saw it with our own eyes.

Gary was just beginning to see purpose in his life when he was struck with terminal cancer at the age of thirty-nine.

When I found out I had this cancer I was like, okay Lord, I know You didn't bring me all this way for nothin' and there's gotta be a point behind this and I'm ready for it. Is there a testimony here that I need to give? Do I need to touch someone in a way that You can use me? Whatever it is, let Your will be done. I'm ready. I can do this.

I'm ready. I can do this. Astonishing. The man had just found out he was dying. He had just discovered how little control he had over things. The angel had both of his shoulders on the ground; the three-count was finished. And Gary said, *I'm ready. I can do this.*

In interview after interview people told us their purpose was tied to what they did for others. Annie said she found her purpose and joy in raising her children: "They're such a joy to me. They're so good to me, and my grandchildren." William M. said, "My family has been the greatest joy I've ever had in my life." He said providing his daughters with a college education might have been the most important thing he ever did. "I've been very proud of all that. I raised my family and did good with what I did." Louise O. saw the accomplishment of her purpose in "raising my children as a single mom" while Mildred pointed to raising her son "the way I raised him."

David D. found his purpose in "just providing for my family—giving them a home, a school, a life." James A. found his purpose in his family and in the activities at his Moose Lodge, especially Moose Haven, a home for foster children.

To Carl, his purpose was simple. "Everybody who's young and ambitious wants to build themselves, of course. But I never desired to be important, well known, or wealthy. . . . The only thing that I ever really took pride in is being known as an honest and a good man. And, if my friends are telling the truth, I accomplished that." Even so, when we spoke with him, he wasn't quite at peace in feeling his purpose has been fully accomplished. "I've been married and divorced. Had three children. My children won't speak to me today. That's killing me."

"How Much Better Can It Get?"

One of the things Kenneth valued most was helping other people, and he lived his life accordingly. He said, "I was able to mow other people's grass, to fix other people's stuff, with or without pay. I didn't care. We were blessed, we've always been blessed financially and we'd like to share the wealth. If you had a flat tire on the interstate, we'd stop and help you." A comment must be inserted here: it was clear from visiting with Kenneth in his home that he was not financially "rich" by a lot of people's standards, but he still viewed his family as being blessed financially.

So then, one of the great joys of Kenneth's life is seeing that his son Paul shares his generous spirit: "We had a mentally handi-

capped fellow coming to church. And they had a special meeting one Tuesday and Paul was there. He got there at the same time that Sam, the special fellow, got there in a cab. Well, Sam didn't have money for the cab fee, never did. So I heard later that Paul took care of it and carried Sam home after the meeting. How much better can it get?"

"How much better can it get?" Just let that soak in for a few minutes. Most fathers I've heard say this are either basking in their child's financial success or competitive accomplishments. I might have even said this myself on the day I realized all of my children had obtained good jobs, with health insurance benefits. This father's greatest source of joy is in seeing his young son, now in his early twenties, have compassion and grace in helping someone.

It was truly overwhelming. We could include quotes from almost every one of the people we interviewed regarding purpose in life. Facing imminent death, the slate was cleared and these people could see what really mattered. It was people. And it was God. In most of the cases where people talked about their purpose being to help people, they cited their motivation as coming from their faith. Whether Unitarian, Jewish, or Christian, they reported that the love that motivated them to be others-focused came from God.

We tried to set aside our own expectations and values as we listened in the interviews and later read and reread the transcripts. To be honest, however, we did have some expectations about what we might hear. We were surprised at how little people talked about professional or work-related accomplishments. Harold M. was one of the most respected architects in the city and designed numerous significant structures in the community. He had been retired for about twenty years when we spoke with him. "I guess the [building] I'm most proud of is the Municipal Auditorium . . . That thing was set up to seat ten thousand people. Anyway, that's one thing I did, and I did some others, too. And most of the others I've done have been razed, they've been knocked down." It's a ready-made metaphor. What could be a more solid, more permanent thing to devote your career to than major downtown buildings? Yet most of them didn't even outlast their architect. On the other hand, Harold spent much of our interview talking about the relationships that gave shape to his life—relationships of eternal import.

Even in the relatively few cases where people talked about their work as being a core part of their purpose, they seemed to reach a point when they recognized that the buildings would be razed or that sometimes work organizations ask things of us that just aren't worth it.

There were four exceptions to the rule that our interviewees didn't talk much about their professional lives. Two were pastors, one was a nurse, and one founded a recovery center for addicts. In each case, their work was directly about caring for people. Their work seemed to be an application of Jesus' admonition that all of the law is fulfilled by truly "loving God and loving people" (see Matt. 22:34–40).

This is not to say your vocation, work, and profession is not, or should not, be important. Providing food for others, providing health care, manufacturing automobiles, teaching, providing for the public safety, and performing countless other endeavors are vital to all our lives. With so much of our lives being spent at work, there is a great need in society for people to align their life's purpose with their work. But what is irrefutable is that "purpose in life," the *why* question, is much, much bigger than work.

As Lee sat in his room at the Alive Hospice facility he observed,

> There's people right outside that hall in a whole lot worse shape than I am. Those people right there might not make it through the day. Personally I hope I'm going to, and maybe, through tomorrow, but, I mean, I don't know. Life isn't a practice. It's the only one you're going to get. And then, who knows what's going to happen? Hopefully something better, but I know after being in that hospital, there's more people in need than me. . . . I've got a dollar, and this guy ain't got nothing, no food? Maybe I need to help him more and not worry about getting another dollar.

Christine was at a similar point in her thinking. "I think the next thing is that while I'm here and as long as I can, I'll do whatever I can. Pray for people, even if I don't talk to them, even if I never knew them, to encourage them. To talk to them if they're in trouble or distress to help calm them down."

Far from believing themselves to be at the end of their usefulness, Christine, Lee, and many other interviewees seemed to believe their purpose was as relevant as ever.

The 1967 movie *Bonnie and Clyde* told the story of one of the most ruthless gangs of murderers and bank robbers in American history. A 1934 FBI report describes how Bonnie and Clyde, along with their accomplices, became the prime suspects in thirteen cold-blooded murders, as well as numerous kidnappings, bank robberies, and auto thefts.

As the movie approaches its end—a very violent end for Bonnie and Clyde—a poignant scene plays out between the two of them. In the dim light of a motel, Bonnie says to Clyde:

> Oh baby, I've got the blues so bad . . .
> I thought when we first went out,
> We were really goin' somewhere . . .
> But this is it—we're just goin', huh?

What a tragedy. To spend your life becoming famous, maybe even rich, thinking you're really going somewhere. Only to realize, as the end approaches, that you weren't really going anywhere, you were just goin'! That's enough to give anyone the blues. Maybe Bonnie and Clyde knew *what*, *where*, *how*, *who*, and *when*, but they didn't know *why*.

People are slow to give explicit, deep thought to questions like "Why are you here?" and "What is your purpose in life?" Most of the hospice patients we talked with had not seriously "wrestled with the angel" to discover their purpose in life until after they learned of their nearness to death. When they began the process of their own near-to-death experience, this question moved to the top of the list. Why don't more healthy, thriving, in-the-prime-of-life people, even young people, resolve this question and then use the answer to guide them through a life of meaning? We do need to get this right. The stories we heard have motivated us to do some deep thinking about what "right" looks like.

What if That Is What It's All About?

In the late 1940s Larry LaPrise wrote one of the most widely known songs in the world. "The Hokey Pokey"[4] remains a worldwide favorite of children and childlike adults. The song's lyrics lend themselves to dance as well as song—shaking your feet and turning around.

A few years back I saw a T-shirt that suggested this startling possibility:

The Hokey Pokey: What if That Is What It's All About?

That can stop you in your tracks if you haven't done any serious, personal thinking for yourself. We tell all of the students who come to our university that we believe they were created by God for a purpose in life. And we don't believe it's just any purpose or that you can choose from a list with the help of a counselor. We believe it's one specific purpose and if you can discover that purpose, whatever it might be, you will lead a life of productivity, accomplishment, and joy. Also, we don't believe God would create you for an important purpose and then just sit back and observe. We believe God is with us and has endowed every person with a set of unique gifts, talents, and passions that, when developed, will enable one to enact his or her purpose. So our university becomes a place where students are encouraged to continue to discover their purpose and passions in life and where the faculty, staff, and other students are committed to helping one another develop their gifts and talents so they become transformed in all they were created to be. We strive to produce students who demonstrate that the Hokey Pokey is decidedly not what it's all about.

Chapter 6

RECONCILIATION

Tammy's first marriage was short and not very happy. They were wealthy enough—she said they had "everything" from a material standpoint—but both she and her husband were addicted to drugs, and so they found no real happiness in their union. After thirteen years they went their separate ways.

Twelve years later, Tammy learned she was dying. Though she hadn't seen or heard from her first husband in years, he was among the first people she called after her diagnosis. "I called him and I apologized to him for anything I might have done to hurt him," she said.

Tammy was one of many interviews whose thoughts turned to reconciliation when they understood they weren't long for this world. The hurts of the past—hurts received, hurts caused—were undeniable facts. But they weren't the most important facts. Truer were the facts of love and restoration and hope.

The reaction of Tammy's husband wasn't atypical either:

"He didn't want to talk about it," she said. He wasn't staring down death, after all. He didn't feel the same urgency she felt.

Clydell was a bachelor and had been separated from his very large family for many years. Nobody was mad at anybody; it's just that when he was a younger man, Clydell felt the need to do things his own way. "I stayed away for a while . . . just to be a man by my own skin, my own issues. I just wanted, I guess, to be myself for a while, you know, so I can figure and work things out."

Clydell's "while" away turned into years, and he lost touch with most of his nine brothers and sisters, not to mention aunts and cousins. When he checked into hospice, however, they asked him for a relative's phone number, and Clydell gave them one aunt's telephone number. It wasn't long before the aunt rounded up the entire family. "They just been coming all out of the woodwork and everywhere," Clydell said.

It was beautiful to see. It was a picture of grace, really. Clydell had given his family no reason to reach out to him. And after so many years, Clydell would have felt strange about reaching out to them, assuming he even had their phone numbers. But they "came out of the woodwork" to be with him in his hour of need.

"I'm glad to come inside after all these years," Clydell said. "It's been a beautiful journey, and soon it will come to an end. Ain't nothing like life." Truer words were never spoken. Ain't nothing like life.

Not all of our interviewees were as fortunate as Clydell. Many suffered rifts with family members that hadn't been reconciled and most likely never would be this side of heaven. William E. mourned bitterly the fact that he would never again see his thirteen-year-old son. The boy was four the last time they saw each other. "I always thought that when he came of age he would know and he would understand, but now it doesn't look like I'm going to be there for it," said William. That was one of the saddest things we heard anybody say: the realization that he waited too late. He would never know a time when his son would understand his actions.

The truth, of course, is that if William were to live to be a hundred, there's a good chance his son would never understand why William abandoned him. The enforced passivity of a hospice bed was terribly sad, but no sadder than the preceding nine years of passivity when William had the opportunity to move toward his son and chose not to.

Thomas D. was another man who found himself longing for a reconciliation that seemed unlikely. As a young man, he struggled to find work in New York. He attended truck-driving school, but because he wasn't a member of a union, he couldn't find work in his chosen field and found himself instead in a series of menial jobs—washing dishes, busing tables, and so forth. It was no easy task providing for a wife and four sons that way.

At last Thomas gave up on New York and decided to come south, where he could get a good job without being part of a union. There was just one catch: his wife didn't want to leave. Her mother was in New York—not to mention the rest of her life. Thomas told her, "I'm going south. I'll try and get us a house. I'll get us set up, and I'll send for you. If you come, you come. If you don't, I'm sorry for you." With that, he literally was "off to join the circus." He traveled with the carnival for the next few years.

His wife never came. She and the boys stayed in New York, and she raised them without their father.

Thomas had recently reestablished contact with his sons by phone, but those twenty years of absence were weighing on him. When we asked him what had been his biggest disappointment in life, he said, "Myself . . . what I've done to my sons. It dwells on me, what I did. I could have sent birthday cards on birthdays. I could have sent Christmas cards. But I didn't."

After moving south, Thomas got involved with a second woman whose irrational jealousy kept him from his sons. "I thought I was so in love with her that I totally ignored my four sons for her," he said. "That's my biggest shame right there."

The irony is that when we asked Thomas what he was proudest of, he didn't hesitate: he was proudest of the sons and wife he had abandoned. "Even without me, they never got into trouble. Not one of them ever got into any trouble. She held them together, and I'm most proud of her for that, and proud of them, because they don't turn their back on me, and I completely ignored them for twenty years. I mean, they grew up without a dad."

At long last, Thomas was starting to take the initiative to communicate with his sons. He was dictating letters into a tape recorder, and his social worker was going to have them typed up for him. "I'm going to explain to them what I did and why I did what I did, and how I feel about what I've done, and take it from there."

Thomas was using the last of his life force to reconcile with his sons. Too little too late? Maybe. But the fact is, all the foolishness and bad choices that kept him from doing this sooner seemed a distant memory, and he wanted to make things as right as he could. After ignoring his sons for twenty years, now he was totally focused on them. They were his greatest joy. His distance from them was his greatest regret and disappointment. Reestablishing communication with them, as difficult as that must have been, became his top priority. Perhaps he was seeing life through a lens that we, the healthy and thriving, don't use often enough.

———

Reconciliation is the first cousin of forgiveness. In order to be genuinely reconciled to others, we have to be willing both to forgive and to seek forgiveness. Sometimes reconciliation is difficult because both parties feel the other has committed the greater wrong. Each party waits for the other to initiate reconciliation, and the result is an ongoing standoff. Other times, both parties agree which side is more guilty, but while the aggrieved party waits for the offending party to initiate reconciliation, the offending party lets embarrassment and/or pride keep him or her from initiating.

People on their deathbeds don't have time or energy for all the fine moral calculations that keep reconciliation from happening. They go after reconciliation like it's the most important thing in the world. Because, of course, it is.

Seeing the ardor with which our interviewees sought reconciliation reminded us of a truth we know but don't always live: Strong, healthy relationships aren't about meeting people halfway. They're about all parties being willing to take 100 percent responsibility for the relationship. If you're committed to taking full responsibility for a relationship, you're going to take the first step in reconciliation.

The main ingredient in reconciliation between people is the same required for reconciliation between people and God: grace. A gracious response is not a natural human response. What is natural is to hold on to your rights, to argue your point, and try to win, to hold the other person accountable. Thankfully, God doesn't treat us that way. He simply sets aside all that separates us, always desiring to be reconciled to us, no matter what we've done to create a gap.

In Gary's story, we saw how a man's reconciliation to God resulted in his desiring to be reconciled to the people he had estranged—his son in particular. Gary had lived life "his way."

I came from a good family and my parents did everything they could for me. I was just hardheaded and decided to do things on my own, my way, regardless of the damage I left . . . [and on] that path the damage I left, how wide and how long . . . there was nothing that meant anything to me. . . . I was in and out of trouble, accumulated eleven years in prison. I was going nowhere, big circle . . . doing a lifetime of stupidity, in and out, not ever taking the time to address what was bothering me that made me do the

things I did. It was always easier to say, "Well I'm an alcoholic." It was a convenience to me. Every time I got in
trouble I'd blame everybody else but myself. I'd blame my
family, blame "somebody did me wrong," this and that,
you know, just as long as the truth was behind me. My
nickname used to be "Little Evil," and I was every bit of
that, and I tried to be every bit of that.

Finally, Gary reached his breaking point—the point where
he could no longer depend on his own resources—and everything changed.

I got to the point, I couldn't live with myself anymore.
I mean, I did so many things, burnt so many bridges. I just
got tired of existing, I mean, 'cause that's all I was doing
was existing. I wasn't living life, not the way I was supposed to, I mean, I didn't even have a concept how we
were supposed to live life. . . . I had my own way of thinking, a world according to Gary and that's that.

One thing I can say I'm grateful to the AA program
[for] is it made me realize there was a void in my life that
needed to be filled. And I, it took me to come to the realization that the void was lacking God. Once I realized I
needed some spirituality in me, boy! And what even blew
my mind even more was realizing I, you, have spirituality
in you already to begin with—it's just up to you to reach
in there and get it. I accepted Jesus Christ as my Lord and
Savior. I got involved with the Nashville Rescue Mission.
I'd never seen such God-dedicated men in my life over
there. I mean, I wasn't that nice, I wasn't a good person,
my mom could even tell you that. I wasn't nothin' nice.

I couldn't be trusted. I'd lie to you, steal from you, whatever, to get Gary's way.

I dedicated myself . . . to keep that walk with God going, no matter what I went through, placing Him first in my life. And the things that I was being taught about the promise of the Bible were working, first time in my life they were working. A man over there, James Overton, was my counselor, gentleman of a Southern Baptist fire-and-brimstone preacher. He just stuck to me like glue. He knew I wanted it. He had seen it in me that I wanted it, and Bud Hoffman, the director of the place, he seen I wanted it. The two of them pushed me to limits I never thought capable of being pushed to. I stuck with it, and I thank God to this day that my heart wasn't so hardened that I was able to learn again, actually open myself up to learn.

Gary's behavior for most of his life did nothing but create distance between himself and others. There was a deep need for reconciliation in his life—reconciliation to his family, reconciliation to a host of people, and reconciliation to God. Having been reconciled to God, he turned his attention to his seven-year-old son. When asked what he was most proud of, Gary's response was immediate:

"The birth of my son. He's in Nebraska. I haven't seen him since he's been three. Me and my ex-wife just do not communicate. . . . Like I said, I used to be nothin' nice, I couldn't be trusted, but it was better that way because I want . . . that when he asks me 'Daddy,' that I'm worth bein' called Daddy."

Gary was a really tough guy, but as he faced the end of his life at the age of forty, he revealed what was really important to him—to be called "Daddy" by his estranged seven-year-old son. He said seeing his son before his transformation would have been "morally damaging" to the boy, "and I couldn't do that before." Now, in his short remaining days, he says he really wanted to see his son—"We're working on it, I'm working real hard on it."

If he was unable to see his son, he had a backup plan.

I write him two letters a week and I store them. I got money orders, all kinds of stuff in these letters. I'm workin' it out where he can't get them 'til he's sixteen or seventeen years old where he'll be able to realize that I was there and that I was writing the letters. I wasn't ready to be a father. Don't hate me for that but I wanted to be a father you deserved to have because you're that special.

With Gary, we yearned for his reunion with his son. But Gary had an even greater longing—a longing he knew would be fulfilled, and soon. When asked what came next for him, he said, "Oh, glory—definitely. Living in a mansion. I'm ready to live in a mansion my Father has built for me up there, walk the streets of gold, be able to walk up to my dad and say hi to him, you know, and seeing people that I haven't seen, or thought I'd never see again because of my actions."

Gary's actions through most of his life pushed people away. He once thought it was too late to draw near to any of those people again. But he was reconciled to God, and as a result, he looked forward to repairing all those relationships he threw away. What a sweet place to be.

Chapter 7

LOVING PEOPLE

Although they were not included in "the 104" that we interviewed, we learned a powerful lesson from Robert and Julia. It was just two hours after Julia, his beloved wife and the mother of their two teenage children, died. When I arrived at their temporary residence to drive them to the airport, my friend Robert took me aside and told me he read in the newspaper that I would be giving the commencement speech at Belmont University's graduation ceremony the next day. He turned to me with an intensity I'll never forget and said, "Well, here's your speech, Bob. You tell those kids life is short and you tell them to find somebody to love and hold on to them." Then he said, "Now, you go home and you hug Judy. And when she says, 'Okay, that's enough,' and tries to push away, don't let her go. Don't let her go."

I took my friend's advice. I took his message to Belmont's graduates. And I also went home and hugged Judy a little longer than she thought necessary.

The soon-departed we spoke with were clearly focused on, if not obsessed with, loving people. For some it was woven into the fabric of their lives early on. To others, their focus on loving others was a response to their near-to-death circumstances. Either way, loving others was on their minds, right up there with loving God.

When the Pharisees were trying to trap Jesus, one of them, a lawyer, asked Him which of the laws was most important. The Pharisees' hope was that whichever commandment Jesus picked, they could then argue for some other law He didn't name. Jesus' response surely had the lawyer walking away shaking his head in confusion. He said, "'You shall love the Lord your God with all your heart, and with all your soul, and with all your mind.' This is the great and foremost commandment." But He didn't stop here. "The second is like it, 'You shall love your neighbor as yourself.' On these two commandments depend the whole Law and the Prophets" (Matt. 22:37–40).

There it is: the whole Law and the Prophets in two commandments—love God, love your neighbor. Annie was obviously paying attention. When we asked her what her one message to the world would be, she answered, "First I would say put the Lord first. And every day [you're] upon His place, just trust Him. Just trust the Lord. And, to be loved, you just love. I guess that's because I've loved everybody."

A couple that was included in the interviews of "the 104" was Larry and Julia. Larry and Julia's life together was a beautiful love story—a love story lasting fifty-nine years. Julia was suffering from ALS—Lou Gehrig's disease. At the time of our interview, she could no longer talk, except through a computer that could say what she typed. Larry did most of the talking during our interview. And the love and tenderness with which he described his wife was both beautiful and heartbreaking.

> Whatever time we have left, whether it is eighteen months or ten years, we don't know, but we're going to live it fully. And let me tell you, we have enjoyed this last period of time wonderfully. We have had a great experience. And a lot of it is just holding each other and letting each other know how much we love each other. . . . We love to hold each other and touch. Julia loves to be held and I love that too. It's just that we don't want to be away from [each other]. We want to be together because we just love each other and care about each other so much.

Larry went on to say, "It's my joy to be with her at this present time and in this condition." Julia, remember, was unable even to talk, much less "do anything" for Larry. But she was still Julia, the woman Larry loved for fifty-nine years. And whatever her physical condition, being with her was joy to Larry. Larry's message to the world isn't surprising: "Whoever you love, you go home and hug and tell them how much you love them that day. Don't wait. We've always done that, but we felt the need to tell everybody else because you don't know what's going to happen tomorrow!"

We spoke to Larry after Julia died, and he told us about her last moments. She made a living will identifying the point at which she should be removed from life support. When her disease progressed to that point, the life-support system was removed. Larry sat with Julia holding her hand. As the ventilator was turned off, Julia threw a kiss to Larry and waved good-bye. Larry described it as the most intimate moment he and Julia ever shared. It was just the two of them together as the last of Julia's life on earth flickered away.

Happiness can be so elusive for those of us firmly entrenched in the land of the living. For the soon-departed, it seemed much simpler. Happiness isn't something to be sought after as another accomplishment, another possession, another accolade. Happiness is as near as the nearest loved one—if only we will give ourselves over to loving them and receiving their love.

Nancy emphasized the importance of being proactive in seeking love, and also the importance of a loving environment to a happy life. She said, "Always be in a place and at a time when you're filled with love and happiness, and don't be around anybody that's gonna bring you down from that." Love and happiness do seem to go hand in hand. "Always try to be happy" was Sam's advice. "Be as happy as you can." A lot of people seem to think happiness is something that just happens from time to time—a serendipitous outcome beyond our influence. Both Nancy and Sam make it clear happiness is something we can lay hold of. And they, and the others, directly link loving people to a happy life.

Marianne agreed that happiness is, to a large degree, determined by the love, or the lack of love, surrounding your life. That's why she, like others, recommended you surround yourself with people you love. She was one of many people we spoke with who experienced heartbreak, having lived with a husband who treated her badly before finally getting out of the marriage. Nevertheless, she still believed love was the key to the good life. "If you live with somebody, really love them . . . and live with people that you love. And," she added, "if love ever stops, get away from them. Don't hang in there." While this may not be the advice you or I would give, it was spoken by one with the experience to back it up, so we should at least listen to her.

Lena also acknowledged that everything doesn't always go perfectly, but she had a great response to those times. "Love, and don't cry over your mistakes. Don't cry." In essence, she was suggesting we love our way out of our mistakes, but more importantly, that we have the ability to choose: we can choose the passive route of crying over spilt milk, or we can choose to love, knowing that "love covers a multitude of sins" (1 Pet. 4:8).

To Harold G., his near-to-death circumstances were just another reason to love even more. "The most rewarding thing that's happened out of all of this [his illness] is the fact that it has brought our family so much closer. We express our love and our care and it just really brought us so close." He talked about how the time since his terminal diagnosis had been a gift of love, contrasting his lingering death to the sudden deaths of the victims of September 11: "Not that our family has been torn or anything like that—we've always had a good family, [but] . . . September 11, had I died on that date, suddenly, our family wouldn't have been what it is today."

On a separate subject, Harold went on to say, "And secondly, maybe this should have been first of all, this time has given me time to do soul-searching and to make whatever amends that I needed to make in order to prepare for the judgment. And so it's been very rewarding!" Harold just amazed us. He was on the doorstep of eternity—he died very soon after speaking with us—and yet he was expressing gratitude for the rewards of his final days and his satisfaction in leaving behind a more loving family as a consequence of his pain, suffering, and death!

In some cases the concept of love was stated rather softly through words such as *kindness*, *sharing*, and *nice*, but all these are the children of love. Some of Harold M.'s most passionate remarks were related to kindness. "I just think that people oughta be more considerate with others. They oughta be kind and thoughtful." Vicki's view involved what can be described as a "childlike vision" of how things could and should be:

> I think while you're here, I think you should just be kind. Be kind. If everybody—I know it sounds stupid—but if we let the children run this world, wouldn't it be a great place? It'd be such a great place if we let the kids just have it. Let the kids run it, we'd have a great world. And it's gonna be that way again . . . it'll be that way again. I just wish people would be kind to other people. I just wish we'd be nicer and kinder. Yeah, you know, treat other people like you'd like to be treated. I know that sounds cliché, but it's the truth.

Lest you think Vicki was just talking when she said, "it's going to be that way again," remember what Jesus said when His disciples complained about the children crowded around Him: "Let the little children come to me, and do not hinder them, for the kingdom of heaven belongs to such as these" (Matt. 19:14 NIV). Vicki was articulating a vision of the kingdom of heaven, where love will be in the ascendancy—where people will be kind and treat others as they themselves would want to be treated.

Nancy said, "It's such a shame that we are so mean. Little people get under our skin and it spoils a whole life." What a great (and accurate) phrase—"It spoils a whole life." Nancy continued. "And it's not worth it. But I think if you're around people that have a smile and all, then you'll take home that smile and then someone will see you . . . and that's how I see it."

Love and happiness aren't likely to come if you just wait around for them. They are most likely to come through a proactive seeking. We are also taught through these conversations that we have a choice regarding how we think and feel about love and happiness. Think of the thousands of images the media throws at us in their attempt to convince us we can't be happy without their product or unless we think as they do. The reality is these marketers don't really care about us. They just want us to convince ourselves we shouldn't be happy until we have their product, that it can't be love unless you buy this for her. The interviewees who seemed the most in love and the happiest didn't let others define happiness for them—they did it for themselves.

Love was coming at us from every direction in our interviews—love given, but also love received. Beverly spoke about how blessed she felt to receive love. "I feel like I am so blessed because I have his two children and three of the grandchildren that love me so much, you know most stepmoms are not blessed that way." And for Mary T., joy was defined as "being loved."

Lena, after telling us to love people, reminded us, "Love yourself. That's very important. I just love myself." Some people immediately recoil at this notion of self-love. But love of self comes highly recommended by psychologists and biblical teachers alike. After all, the Bible teaches us to love others by challenging us to love them the way we love ourselves: "You shall love your neighbor as yourself; I am the LORD" (Lev. 19:18). When a verse ends with "I am the Lord," it's a clue that we ought to listen. Love others as you love yourself; clearly God doesn't intend for us to wallow in self-loathing if self-love is the baseline for the way we love others. Loving self doesn't have to be selfish. Psychologists (not to mention casual observation) tell us that those who have low self-esteem and place a low value on their own lives don't know how to value others highly. The admonition to love ourselves is really just an extension of Marianne's advice to surround ourselves with love.

This has been a pretty random—and somewhat arbitrary—sampling of the love-related messages we heard from our interviewees. In truth, just about everyone had something to say on the subject, to the point they almost seemed clichéd. Almost, but not quite. There's a reason so many people were talking about love: because it's the most important thing in the world. I thought of Paul McCartney's song "Silly Love Songs" as I listened to yet another person speak about the importance of love:

You'd think that people would have had enough of silly love songs.
But I look around me and I see it isn't so.
Some people wanna fill the world with silly love songs.
And what's wrong with that, I'd like to know?
Cause here I go, again
I love you! I love you!
I love you! I love you![1]

There they went again, over and over. Love is that important.

~~~~

First Corinthians 13:1–8 is the most familiar meditation on love in all of Scripture.

If I speak with the tongues of men and of angels, but do not have love, I have become a noisy gong or a clanging cymbal.

If I have the gift of prophecy, and know all mysteries and all knowledge; and if I have all faith, so as to remove mountains, but do not have love, I am nothing.

And if I give all my possessions to feed the poor, and if I surrender my body to be burned, but do not have love, it profits me nothing.

Love is patient, love is kind and is not jealous; love does not brag and is not arrogant, does not act unbecomingly; it does not seek its own, is not provoked, does not take into account a wrong suffered, does not rejoice in unrighteousness, but rejoices with the truth; bears all things, believes all things, hopes all things, endures all things.

Love never fails.

Love never fails. When we conducted the 104 interviews that were the basis for this book, we were talking to people for whom all earthly measures had failed. Their bodies had failed them; modern medicine had failed them. They were in hospice care because, quite literally, all else failed; the worst-case medical scenario turned out to be the case. But save for a few of the people we spoke with, the result wasn't despair, but a turning toward that which could not fail: the love of God, the love of family and friends, their own love for those around them.

Kathleen put it best: "Love never fails. If you show love, love calms, love drives out fear, love instills comfort. Love draws people to you. . . . But I believe that love never fails . . . if you genuinely love then it will never fail you—and a smile will help too."

Leaving a Legacy

The word legacy *communicates the idea of leaving something behind. According to Merriam-Webster it's something "transmitted by or received from an ancestor or predecessor or from the past." While we didn't ask people any specific questions regarding their legacy, we did get some unsolicited answers anyway. Reitha told us, "My husband's been writing a book. He said he wanted to leave a legacy. And I thought,* Well, what can I leave? I leave my children. *That's what I'm most proud of, being a mother." Margaret F. was so proud of her grandchildren—"I've got one in California, one in Florida, and two in Tennessee." She went on with great pride to tell us stories about them. The message Margaret wanted her grandchildren to remember endowed them with a priceless legacy. "[I would want them to] just remember how much I loved 'em, and for them to carry on." A legacy is what you leave behind, and Margaret left them love. Margaret would have appreciated what Shirley H. said on the subject. "The only thing I ever say that's gonna last for any amount of time is the love that you have for other people. You love the ones closest to you and you stand by them through everything and you don't give up!"*

Chapter 8

LAUGHING AT LIFE

In Victorian England there were many odd professions that no longer exist, but one of the oddest was surely the occupation of "professional mourner." Families of the deceased would pay mourners to swell the ranks of the bereaved at a funeral and to set an appropriately somber tone; these professional mourners would go from funeral to funeral of people they didn't know, dressed in black and looking very—well—mournful.

Why on earth did the Victorians think they needed professional help to mourn their dead at a funeral? Well, think about it. Don't you have a hard time knowing exactly how to act at a funeral? Sometimes you don't know whether to laugh or cry (and, of course, you often end up doing both). Everybody knows a story about somebody getting tickled at a funeral and laughing at an inappropriate time. What's that about? Part of it is the emotional stress of a loved one's death. Death evokes such strong emotions they burst their way out any way they can—tears or laughter or something between.

But some of the laughter you see at funerals, memorial services, wakes, and visitations is genuine celebration of a life. We tell stories about the deceased as a way to honor them, and often those stories are funny.

I'll never forget the story of the last fender bender (the last of many) that finally resulted in Granddad Claude getting his driver's license revoked. He rear-ended a car at a traffic light (which, in his defense, had turned green). When the police officer asked him to explain himself, Claude said, "Well, the light was green, and he should have gotten out of the way—I needed to get going!"

Stories like that really seem to flow when a loved one is dying or departed. The laughter is no disrespect to the dead, but a rejoicing in their life. Our attitudes have changed since the day of the professional mourner. Perhaps the people of New Orleans are onto something with the raucous street parties that accompany their funerals.

We heard a lot of laughter in our conversations with the soon-departed—more than you might expect from people in such dire circumstances. But you might say the laughter was *because* of the dire circumstances, not *in spite* of them. Laughter makes people feel better, and these were people who definitely needed to feel better. There weren't all that many true jokes told—though Melvin couldn't resist trotting out that old chestnut from *The Pink Panther*, the one where the man asks, "Does your dog bite?"

Nancy vividly described what laughter meant in her life. She said she loved "to be in a room with loving people; anyone having a real good time. You can just grab it in the air, you know? I like to be where there's laughter. I can be really down about something and be invited to a party or something and it will lift me right up. I'll listen to that laughing and that means a lot to me. I love to hear it!" Mildred B. had a similar take on laughter. "The important thing is making people laugh. I really enjoy that, and especially when I can laugh about me!"

There are many different kinds of laughter, of course. At one end of the spectrum is sardonic, sarcastic laughter that tears people down. At the other end is the life-affirming laughter of a joyful heart. The difference is illustrated in the life of Sarah from the book of Genesis. When the angel announced that Sarah, a ninety-year-old woman, would be having a baby, Sarah laughed in mockery. But a year later Sarah did indeed have a baby, and her sardonic laughter was transformed into laughter of pure joy. The joke was on her, and she couldn't be any happier about it.

We didn't get a lot of sardonic laughter from the soon-departed. Their energies were devoted elsewhere. To a certain extent, perhaps there were people for whom laughter was a sort of "whistling in the dark"—something pleasant to get their minds off the dark mysteries that lay ahead. But I really don't believe there was a lot of that. The laughter we saw was life affirming.

Take, for instance, the family who took in John G. as he neared his departure. They laughed as they told the story of how this developmentally disabled man used his police scanner to get into all kinds of situations. "He carried an actual scanner, so he would get to wrecks [on his bicycle] before the police department, and he would be out there directing traffic before they would get there. He heard of President Carter coming to town and of the police escorting him. Well, he got in the middle of this escort and was taken in by the Secret

Service, but to him it was okay because he was supposed to escort the president." That funny little story told a great deal about who John was. Now that John is gone, that story is an epitaph, a laughing epitaph that says, "Here lies John, who always wanted to help . . . and who always seemed to get himself into a mess . . . and whom everybody loved anyway."

"Oh, Well"

I don't know his name, but I do recognize the face of this nearby resident of a retirement home as he strolls through campus from time to time. Time may have changed him in the couple of years since I last saw him, but I would recognize him immediately by his cap, his campaign-style buttons, and his shirt that summarized a life philosophy in two words: "Oh, well." During the time he was most active in visiting campus he would talk with anyone who approached him. I had the inevitable conversation with him one day myself. "What's the story behind 'Oh, well?'" I asked. He told me he thought most of us took ourselves and our lives too seriously. He said life is serious, but we're not in control. So when things don't go just as we've planned them, we need to learn to simply say, "Oh, well" and move on. I would have liked to learn more, but I was late for an appointment.

The "Oh, well" guy really attracted some attention and generated some thinking at the height of his campus activism. One men's fraternity even adopted "Oh, well" as their theme for the year and plastered it on their caps, T-shirts, and other promotional items. My first response to this was mild concern that this wasn't exactly a deep commitment to brotherly love and academic excellence. But then I thought of all the other possibilities for fraternity themes and decided they could have done much worse.

One of the boldest questions we asked everyone was, "What comes next for you?" I'm glad I don't get asked that question every day. A common response to this and some of the other really tough questions was to use humor to avoid, or soften, the real answer. Mary W. said, "I have no idea, unless it would be my funeral." When we asked Annie, "What comes next for you?" she pretended to be alarmed and said, "Are you taking my oxygen?" After a laugh, she said, "I'll be going home, so that will be the next thing." Jane responded to the same question by saying "Above . . . I hope. Up above, not down below!" Others, like Susan, had even higher expectations. "One whale of a party. I have so many friends in heaven!" She got it. Life in its fullness—whether here or in heaven—is marked by gladness and good fellowship, by laughter.

We also observed a pattern of people using humor to soften the atmosphere when they realized that things were getting really serious. It was as though they were saying, "*Life is serious, but I may be taking myself too seriously.*" Christine told us that after her husband died, she realized everything had changed:

I was never sick, but I started getting this disease after he died. I didn't understand why till later and it was real clear that I didn't care whether I lived or died, because he wasn't supposed to go anywhere without me. . . . I told the Lord I can pray for others, but I just can't go on anymore, Lord. I'm too tired to fight for myself. And I said, [Lord] I want to see You so bad. I said, I miss my husband.

And then she ended with an endearing touch of humor: "I have so many things I need to yell at him about!" It's as if she suddenly realized she was being intensely introspective and personal, and needed to soften things for herself and her visitor.

There was a similar moment with Harold M. Harold graduated from the School of Architecture at Clemson University, but spent his career working and living in the heart of University of Tennessee country. We were speaking just a few days before Clemson was scheduled to play Tennessee in the Peach Bowl football game. We had just been talking about his cancer, how much he missed his departed wife, how you need to be very careful not to hurt people—some pretty heavy stuff. As he paused I asked him, "Is there anything else you would want the whole world to know about what is important in life? He paused thoughtfully and then said, "Well, I sure hope Clemson beats UT!" This application of humor may just be a reminder that when we get too serious for too long, humor can provide a welcome retreat.

As we approached the early interviews we were a little worried that we would encounter some really tough, uncomfortable moments where we would need to console and reassure the soon-departed. We were wrong. In actuality what we encountered were people who went out of their way to try to make *us* feel comfortable. Some, like Rodney, may have been taking on too much responsibility in this regard. Rodney said the steady stream of visitors who came to see him was participating in "the final viewing." His wife, Dena, told us Rodney recently confided to her, "I gotta hurry up. After all these people coming to see me I gotta hurry up and die and not disappoint them!" She went on to tell us Rodney said, "I'm so glad we got to see them, but I gotta make them feel good." She said, "We joke like that all the time!"

One day in church a minister made reference to the fact that Kenneth "didn't have much time left with them." Kenneth, who was present, told us, "It got real quiet." There was some crying: "Even a couple of males started to dab their eyes." Kenneth went on to say his comment was, " 'Look, I've got good news! You all's life expectancy has gone up. The doctor has told me to quit driving, so you all are now safe again!' "

Kenneth used his humor to address issues that may seem morbid to those who aren't facing death. When it came time for an elder to announce to the church Kenneth was coping with ALS, Kenneth relates, "I told the elder 'Tell them I don't want their pity. I don't want their sympathy and all that.' Well, he gets out there and tells them, 'Kenneth does not want you to treat him or mistreat him anymore than you're doing now. Everybody knows you'll mistreat Kenneth.' " He also described his thinking as he was planning his own memorial service: "We found a new preacher a year ago. After two or three sermons and a couple of get-togethers, I liked him. I liked his style. So I go up to him and I said, 'Stu, you've not been here six months, but I like your style. I like the way you treat people. How about doing my memorial service being that you're only here for six months? That way, your rebuttal time won't be so long! 'Cause [if you don't] I'll get some old coot up there that's known me for thirty years and he's gonna play out all this bad stuff and tell all this bad stuff I've been through. . . . No, I want it happy and joyous.' "

Interactions between patients and doctors were often touched with humor. Maxine reported, "The first time I ever went to see him [her doctor] he asked me what was wrong with me. He said, 'How do you feel?' I said, 'Like ninety-nine miles of bad road!' He said, 'I must have missed that class in medical school because I don't know what that is.'"

Mary T. mixed humor with poignancy. She told us when she was first diagnosed and "Dr. Cohen told me I maybe had about six months, I thought, *Oh, that's just right before graduation*." With two children in the family slated to graduate— one from college and one from high school—she told herself, "I just can't do that. I'm just not going to ruin that and I told [the doctor] that I would try to be strong. . . . So I made it through this graduation." She went on to say she told the doctor who predicted she would die in the spring, "You owe me a summer wardrobe because I gave my summer clothes away in anticipation of not being around for the summer!"

Anna's daughter, Donna, proved that those facing death weren't the only ones who could laugh at death. After talking about the tumors, MRIs, doctors, and pain, Donna said, "So we're just going from day to day. And I tell her you're not going to die today, and tomorrow doesn't look good either!"

The final advice from the soon-departed comes from Christine, a self-confessed practical joker. "We played practical jokes on one another to lighten up the atmosphere. God has a wonderful sense of humor. And laugh, learn to laugh. The experiences that you have now that might seem terrible, the truth is that years from now you will look back and laugh. You will really laugh. And people will think you're crazy, but you will know why you're laughing!"

In 1927 Eugene O'Neill published a now-obscure play called *Lazarus Laughed*. It focuses on the life of Lazarus after he was resurrected by his friend Jesus. It doesn't take much imagination to envision the first questions Lazarus would be asked by his friends and family. "What is death like? What happens on the other side? Tell us where have you been and what did you see?" Could you imagine it in today's world? No doubt Lazarus would be asked to appear on *The Today Show, Good Morning America, Montel, Dr. Phil, Oprah, Letterman, Leno, Hardball, Larry King Live*, and he could be the main feature interview at the Crystal Cathedral. Everyone would want to know the answers to these questions. In O'Neill's dramatization, the first question that came from the friends of Lazarus was, "What is beyond?"

Lazarus's answer first comes in the form of laughter, which mystifies those around him. When they continue to press him, Lazarus responds with a truly cutting question: "O Curious Greedy Ones, is not one world in which you know not how to live enough for you?" Ouch! But his friends are not deterred in their quest for insight. Finally Lazarus responds, "There is only life." In the course of the play it becomes clear that the message is "there is no death"; what we call death is "the fear in between" life on earth and eternal life.[1]

I think that's why so many of the soon-departed we talked to were able to laugh in the face of death. They had begun to understand that death is simply a transition between two lives. And in the face of that joyous realization, who wouldn't laugh?

So laugh. Laugh often, laugh quietly, laugh loudly, laugh to yourself, laugh at yourself, laugh at life, laugh at death, laugh, laugh, laugh. These 104 people, facing imminent death, had peeled away all the outer crust and were looking right into the core of life. And when they did, they found that in living, and in dying, laughter really matters. At the end of the journey, laughter is a sign of a life well lived.

"The Way We Were"

The old Barbra Streisand song "The Way We Were (Memories)" is so powerful. It is tightly linked to the line of thinking that our interviews provoked: "If we had it all to do again, would we? Could we?" We clearly recall a Sunday-morning National Public Radio show that was remembering the life of the wonderful comedian/entertainer Gilda Radner. She became famous for her comedy as an original member of the cast of Saturday Night Live. One of her best-known skits always ended with the phrase "It's always something!"

For Gilda the final "something" was ovarian cancer, which took her life at the much-too-young age of forty-two. As we listened to excerpts of her comedy we found ourselves wiping tears from the laughter.

And then as Gilda, in the character of Rosanne Roseannadanna, belted out the final lines to "The Way We Were," we found ourselves wiping tears of sadness as she closed the program:

> So it's the laughter
> We will remember,
> Whenever we remember
> The way we were.[2]

It really is the laughter that we remember.

Chapter 9

GETTING ALONG

As our conversation with Kenneth progressed, we veered off into topics such as poverty, crime, and war. We discussed the prevalence of prejudice, disrespect, and hate—which is to say, we discussed those problems that rise from our inability to get along. I was reminded of a prayer I heard just a few days earlier: "Lord, we've learned how to fly through the sky at five hundred miles per hour, we've learned how to travel to the moon and back, and we've learned how to clone creation. But we still don't know how to get along with one another. Please teach us." A review of history reveals a pretty bleak track record when it comes to simply "getting along."

Getting along was a major focus for the soon-departed with whom we talked. Life was distilled to its essence for them, and whether by instinct or as the result of long introspection, they let go of grudges and renewed their commitment to loving those who surrounded them. Prejudice, disrespect, and hatred may have swirled in the world outside, but in those hospice rooms, on those deathbeds, love and respect for others carried the day.

One unforgettable conversation was with a daughter and her dying mother. Besides the daughter, there was a "ne'er-do-well" son in the family. He wasn't at his mother's bedside because he was either in jail or rehab. The contrast between the mother's attitude toward that son and the daughter's attitude is an illustration of what I mean when I say the dying are more committed to getting along than the rest of us.

The son had caused the mother all manner of heartache and trouble. She took out loans to pay for rehab. She raised his children for several years. Still, no bitterness was detectable in her voice when she spoke of her son. "We didn't worry about any of it," she said. "All we wanted was what he needed."

The daughter, however, found it harder to let go of her bitterness toward her brother. She went so far as to blame her mother's terminal illness on him. "I have the anger with him because I look back, and would she be where she is right now if she had not had all that stress? But she wouldn't redo anything that she's done."

There is no question that this daughter loved her mother very deeply. But when it came down to it, she couldn't bring herself to honor her mother by loving what her mother loved. She let her own bitterness get in the way. At the end of her life, the mother just wanted to be proud of the son she raised. She knew he was a scoundrel and a mooch. But she was his mother, and she claimed the right of a mother to love her child much more than he deserved. When asked what she was proudest of, she didn't hesitate: "I'm proud of my daughter and her husband and family." Then, after a brief pause she added, "And my son. [I have] to be proud of him." The daughter had given her mother plenty of reason to be proud of her. But the mother needed to be proud of her son, too, even if it took more effort and creativity.

Asked what gave her the most joy, the mother said, "Everybody getting along. You know, the family being peaceful and everything going smoothly. . . . I don't want to leave this world knowing they're at each other's throats."

As much as she loved her mother, as much as she did for her, the daughter withheld the one thing that would have given her mother the greatest joy. She refused to be reconciled with her brother. She refused to let go of her grievances and forgive where her mother forgave. The mother only wanted to leave the world confident her children wouldn't be at one another's throats.

I hesitated even to tell that story. It is not my intention to criticize people who are under such tremendous stress—especially since I've never walked a mile in their moccasins. But I tell it anyway because it makes a very important point. The mother didn't have the strength to hold grudges anymore. Her life was ebbing away, and she refused to waste any of it on bitterness. She seemed to have made a conscious decision to devote her remaining energies to loving and reconciling. She spent the last of her life force on that which builds up and affirms life, not that which tears it down. The daughter, you might say, had too much energy for her own good. While her mother was clutching the last of her life, she was clutching old hurts and jealousies. She was refusing to get along.

A few of our interviewees spoke of their own experience with prejudice and bigotry. Maxine's mother was a Native

American, a member of the Seneca Tribe. Maxine said her mother was proud of her heritage and refused to change her customs or the way she dressed. As a result, the family was subjected to bigotry during the years when Maxine was growing up. "My father followed the harvest, strictly because we had to. They didn't want my mother—she was 'a thieving redskin.'"

But her mother didn't respond to hatred with hatred. "We were not allowed to use the word *hate*," Maxine said, "or if we did, she would hit us with a broom. *Hate* is an ugly word—doesn't even belong in the dictionary. If you don't like something or you don't like someone, don't bother hating them. Just put it in your pocket and forget about it."

Maxine continued, "If [God] is our father, then we are all brothers and sisters."

The Russians Love Their Children, Too

We've created a real paradox in our thinking today about people. On one hand we have become very individual-focused, emphasizing the uniqueness of every person. In the process we have focused on how people are different and then challenged one another to understand, respect, and live with those differences. We go out of our way to not offend others by not imposing ourselves on them. This is a good thing. The negative of emphasizing how we are different is that we find politicians, businesses, and even religious groups that seek to divide us according to those differences and then use their "grouping" as a power base to support their agenda.

The truth is, while people are different from one another, peo-

ple are also very much alike. We hold so much in common. By focusing on what we have in common and how we are alike we have the opportunity to bring people together rather than to divide and keep them apart. In the celebration of our differences, the pendulum seems to have swung away from emphasizing what we actually share with one another and how we are the same. The legitimacy of the golden rule depends on the degree to which we really are like others and want to be treated like they want to be treated.

In the old days of the Cold War between the United States and Russia, much effort was made by both sides to differentiate the people of the two countries from one another to build cohesion for one side or the other. Over time, as the rhetoric cooled and the countries sought to be reconciled, one of the phrases that emerged in the conversation was "The Russians love their children, too!" And indeed they do. And so do the French, the English, the Iraqis, the Mexicans, the Canadians, the Republicans, the Democrats, the Libertarians, the Catholics, the Protestants, the Jews, the Muslims, the Redskin fans, the Yankee fans—you get the idea.

David H. was dying of AIDS. He was pretty hostile to some of our questions, especially when he thought we were trying to get at some specifically religious message. Perhaps his response is not surprising, considering some of the personal attacks he must have endured—some even coming from religious leaders who invoke God's wrath as the cause of his pain and suffering. Contrast that to the core message of God's unconditional love and desire for a relationship with all.

The invitation hymn I responded to as a boy was "Just As

I Am." My God still accepts people, just as they are. It is only through His indwelling, transformative love that any of us will ever be able to stand before Him. What a tragedy when people step in front of God's outstretched arms and become barriers to His glory!

People confronting death seem to become less judgmental as they consider the prospect of their own judgment day. The admonition to "judge not, that you be not judged" (Matt. 7:1 NKJV) rang more loudly than ever. Yes, there will be a judgment day. But we won't be the ones judging; God will. Our interviewees' renewed focus on the grace and mercy they were hoping to receive led them, in turn, to demonstrate more grace and mercy in their relationships with others. Christine said it well:

> The people around you, you can't judge by the cover. There will be people that are in different walks of life and you may not agree with their lifestyle, but the Lord doesn't require you to judge them. He asks you to just love them, pray for them, and help them wherever you can. It'll come from unexpected places.

Christine's remarks really require no comment, but I can't help but add that God doesn't just *ask* that we love others; He *commands* it!

Beverly took that command very seriously:

> Jesus said, "My commandment to you is to love one another," you know, and I think if we love one another it would solve so many problems for everybody. I think it's so hard for people to forgive and love . . . it's hard for people

to love people that they don't think are worthy . . . like people on the street. But you know, who are we to judge their life? We're here to love one another and help one another. That's what Jesus wants us to do.

Gary brought a similar message of love and reconciliation:

We all grow up from different walks and backgrounds. But when it comes down to all this hatred, I mean the main thing for me is . . . get your mind right. We hate in today's society so easy because we don't take the time to communicate to know somebody. Just take the time out to know people. Don't hate 'em 'cause you don't know 'em.

Discussing the conflicts and wars in the world that are driven by religious differences, Gary said,

When it comes down to it, I don't know none of them religions that practice hate, teach hate—not if it's true [to the teachings of the] religion. You read the Koran, the Koran doesn't teach hate. Nowhere, it's not in there. That's man twisting, using the Bible to justify his ignorance, 'cause nowhere in the Koran or anywhere does it tell you to hate somebody. There's no religious faction—the Buddhists, the Hindus—there's nowhere that says hate, hate, hate. There's nowhere that says kill because of hate. You know, it's the governments that do that! Take the time out to know 'em before you pass that kind of judgment, that's the main thing.

Gary's passion was strong on this issue. We should all get as stirred up as Gary did when we see religious teachings meant to bring love, joy, peace, patience, and kindness being misused by people to gain political power and to achieve self-oriented goals. Even though these types of conflicts have dominated wars since the beginning of recorded history, Gary hadn't given up. He's left it in our hands to stop the hate.

———

How we treat one another was clearly on the minds of the soon-departed. I love the way Harold M. put it: "Be careful with people." He didn't mean "guard yourself" or "mistrust others," rather we should be as careful with people as we are with other precious things. He spoke out of a genuine respect for the dignity and ultimate value of everyone. He suggested that much of what we take for granted as trivial may actually, in the end, be what really matters. "You've got to realize what's important and what's the trivia of life. . . . Concentrate on things that are important, and these important things may be considered trivial, in a sense, but they're important as well."

When asked to give an example of what he meant by this, Harold went right to relationships.

Well, just everyday living, the people you're with every day and all that. It's such a common thing that it seems trivial to experience it. You think, *So what, I'll be with you tomorrow.* But this is so important. It's an amazing thing in your life because you're making real impacts on other people and they may not even know it, and they may be making impacts on you, and you don't know it either. I think that this is an important thing. I think people ought to be more considerate with others. They ought to be kind and thoughtful. But anyway, that's something that's amazingly important to your life is dealing with people, and you ought to make that important. Give it a lot of thought and consideration. . . . It takes a long time to learn that sometimes . . . and some people never get it!

What wisdom! You don't know what impact you're making on others. You don't even know what impact they're making on you. So our everyday relationships aren't something to be taken lightly. It is said that familiarity breeds contempt. Harold said just the opposite. On the front porch of eternity, his most familiar people and relationships were the most precious things in the world. "Life is dealing with people, and you ought to make that important."

Leaders have a great responsibility to treat people well at work or in other community settings. Donald was a very successful businessman. He was also the kind of leader for whom we would all like to work. We asked him what about his life made him the most proud. He answered, "I've gotten to this point in my life without having to use anyone, without having trampled anyone, without having to be mean or ruthless—without having to be those kinds of things." That's a wonderful testament to a life well lived. Donald understood what success was.

There's a definite balancing act leaders have in both expressing care and concern while still holding people accountable for excellent performance. But Donald's advice is if you have to err, err on the side of care and concern. This especially makes sense if you frame it in the context of Donald's observation about what really matters: "[The most important thing that I've ever done] is helping people. Helping people that I've met, that I've run across in my life and my business. Teaching people to enjoy life and to get from life what you can and what you want without mistreating people. To [be a good leader] without having to terrify [people] and without having to be an ogre."

Like most businessmen, Donald had a drive to succeed—to do more, to get more. But for Donald, that drive was balanced by a sense of what was really important. "I'm never satisfied with what I get accomplished," he said. "I would like to have done more but on the other side of that once you learn that this life isn't about what you can and can't accomplish then I don't have any major regrets."

Donald's insight that "life isn't about what you can and can't accomplish" elevates people to the very top of the list. People really, really matter. As Harold M. said, we should "be careful with people"!

In saying we should be careful with people, Harold was just expressing what C. S. Lewis said in his sermon "The Weight of Glory." Lewis reminds us that every person we know will someday be either a heavenly being (making us "potential gods and goddesses" is his phrase) or a resident of hell ("a horror and a corruption"). That perspective changes the way we view the people around us.

It is a serious thing, to live in a society of possible gods and goddesses, to remember that the dullest and most uninteresting person you talk to may one day be a creature which, if you saw it now, you would be strongly tempted to worship, or else a horror and a corruption such as you now meet, if at all, only in a nightmare. All day long we are, in some degree, helping each other to one or other of these destinations. It is in the light of these overwhelming possibilities, it is with the awe and the circumspection proper to them, that we should con‐ duct all our dealings with one another, all friendships, all loves, all play, all politics. There are no "ordinary" people. You have never talked to a mere mortal. Na‐ tions, cultures, arts, civilisations—these are mortal, and their life is to ours as the life of a gnat. But it is immor‐ tals whom we joke with, work with, marry, snub and ex‐ ploit—immortal horrors or everlasting splendours. This does not mean that we are to be perpetually solemn. We must play. But our merriment must be of that kind (and it is, in fact, the merriest kind) which exists between people who have, from the outset, taken each other se‐ riously—no flippancy, no superiority, no presumption. And our charity must be a real and costly love, with deep feeling for the sins in spite of which we love the sinner—no mere tolerance or indulgence.[1]

You have never talked to a mere mortal. That's an as‐ tonishing thing to think about. We live in a world where conflict is the norm and tolerance is considered one of the great virtues. Tolerance may be better than conflict, but as Lewis points out, we're setting the bar far too low if toler‐ ance is our goal. We aren't here to tolerate people. We're here to love them, to treasure them, to help them along their way.

The Golden Rule

When we consider what really matters in life, it shouldn't be surprising that some very familiar slogans, phrases, and proverbs step forward. One of the most familiar to all of us is a rule we were taught very early in life, first at home and then at church and school: the golden rule. A form of this rule is stated in the Bible from Leviticus to the New Testament. Probably the most common paraphrase of the golden rule is: "Do unto others what you would have them do to you." In other words, treat people the way you would like to be treated.

As with so many other of the messages in this book, this "rule" is not new to us. In fact, it may be that for many of us we have known it so long we have become somewhat numb to its implications—familiarity can breed contempt. But a fresh examination of this concept, through the words of the soon-departed, has the potential to shake us out of our everyday haze and cause us to see the brilliance of a day lived following this powerful rule.

As we neared the end of our interview with Willie F., she had grown very tired. She told us, "A few minutes seem like hours to me." We promised to wrap up the interview quickly, but we wanted to ask one more question: "What would be your message to the entire world on how to live life?" "I don't know, let's see . . . I'll have to think it over . . . the golden rule . . . I guess that's about as strong [as it gets]. . . . I can't think right now. I'm not thinking very well." In the midst of her struggle to think clearly through the fog surrounding her illness, Willie remembered what really matters: the golden rule. And that's how it should work—when we need direction the most, these core thoughts about what really matter should be so embedded in our being that they emerge as our compass.

As a man of few but meaningful words, Melvin sent a message to his daughter that was short and to the point: "Just to live right. And treat everybody right. That's all, the only thing I know to tell her." What if we all took Melvin's message and acted on it—we lived right and we treated everybody right? This simple change would totally transform the world in which we all live. Perhaps this is an oversimplification. Maybe Melvin's solution is so simple it can't be right. But I'm not willing to give up. I get the feeling Melvin did his part in his lifetime!

Imbedded in the golden rule is the need for a basic respect and understanding of others. A failure of fundamental mutual respect, coupled with the unwillingness to try to understand another's point of view, has created a world of hostility, hate, and killing. The soon-departed seemed to regret they were leaving the world in such a state. Louise O. summed things up this way: "We're all one. We can certainly worship in different ways, we can eat different foods, we can have different beliefs about holidays and so forth, but we're still the same and should treat each other accordingly. Really, the golden rule is kind of it!"

Chapter 10

PEACE—SHIRLEY'S STORY

The outlines of her life sound like a living hell. She was raped at the age of eight. She was an alcoholic by the age of twelve and struggled with the disease for the rest of her life. After she found out her husband was having an affair with her sister, she raised her four children alone, living hand-to-mouth on wages she earned the hard way—in a poultry processing plant.

And yet at the end of life, Shirley was able to say she had no regrets. On the front porch of eternity, she looked back and saw a purpose in it all, and that gave her peace. "I don't fear death," she told me. "There was a time I was scared, afraid. But today I don't fear death. . . . Getting help by drink, I wanted to die. But even though today I carry an uncurable disease, I want to live. Either way. Living my life is joy. If He take my life, it's still joy."

Shirley was paraphrasing the apostle Paul: "For to me, to live is Christ and to die is gain" (Phil. 1:21 NKJV). How many times have I heard those words? But hearing them from a woman in Shirley's circumstances was a life-changing experience for me. Spoken by a woman who overcame both the fear of dying and the fear of life, those weren't just empty words or religious cant.

Shirley knew what it was to feel unloved. Her body was racked with the pain of terminal cancer. And yet what I heard in her voice was a different pain—the pain of deeper hurts from long before. "I never felt I was loved. I would ask why people don't love me. What's wrong? . . . Before I found God, there was no peace in my life. Just living day to day, you know, wanting to die. Wanting to die back then, 'cause life was so screwed up."

In spite of all that pain, however, Shirley also knew the transforming love of God that brings beauty out of ashes:

> Since finding God, it's brought me a peace. Brought a peace. I've got a joy, a happiness. And love. And you know, I was trying to find it in everything else in the world. In drugs, in alcohol, in people. I tried everything, trying to find love until I found the God of my understanding. Then my eyes opened. Then it came like a light. Then I took a look on the insides of me, and that was a great joy too—finding that love on the inside of me.

We heard a lot of religious talk in our interviews. Some of it, to be frank, sounded a little hollow, as if people knew they were supposed to talk about God and Jesus and heaven at the end of life, but hadn't really experienced the things they were talking about. In Shirley, however, it was obvious she was talking about a faith she lived. She tried the route of empty religiosity, and it didn't work: "Going to church, you feel like you should be a part of it. I tried those things but I still feel alone. . . . All my life, I would look for the preacher's God, my daddy's God, my sister's God. But that doesn't happen."

Shirley found God when she came to the end of her own resources and entered Alcoholics Anonymous. There she came to know what she called "the God of my own understanding." She was speaking of the Christian God, to be sure; she wasn't making up a new belief system. But she understood the life-changing power of the God of the Bible for the first time. "I been to the point in my life where I couldn't trust my life," she said. "Couldn't trust myself. But I trusted God." You couldn't hope for a clearer statement of the Christian doctrine that we are saved by God's grace and not our own works.

Talking to Shirley, I got the impression that everything she had done in her life was preparation for this stage of dying well. She had long before learned to place her whole self—body and soul—in the care of the God who loved her. After all, on her own she had very few resources in which to place her trust.

Shirley told the story of a time when she had thirty-two dollars in food stamps to feed four children and herself for a month. Chickens were on sale at the grocery store, so she bought fifteen—one per day for half a month or so.

So okay, we have boiled chicken, baked chicken, chicken with rice, barbecue chicken. Got down to our last chicken. And my son say to me, he say, "Mama, what we going to have today?"

And I said, "Chicken."

He said, "Mama, we ain't got but one."

I say, "We gonna have that chicken."

"What we gonna have tomorrow?"

"Tomorrow ain't here yet. But you know what? God will bless me before this day is over."

When they sat down to eat that last chicken, the phone rang and a friend said she had something to bring to Shirley. She brought a gift of fifty dollars. "I went in there and I told all my kids, I said, 'Don't you see how God moves? Don't you see the miracle?'"

Which is to say, Shirley didn't start putting her trust in God on her deathbed. She had fourteen years to respond to His faithfulness. "All my life I been surrounded by darkness, until I found God. And you know, I just saw a little bit of light. A little bit. And each day I go through a storm, that light would get that bigger, that bigger. Then another storm come in my life, and I endure, then that light get bigger, get bigger."

The light of God's love, ever growing, lit Shirley's way to heaven. And in that light, Shirley was able to see the sufferings of her early life in a whole new way. In the end, God's love banished regret.

I do not regret my past. If I hadn't went through them tough times, I don't believe I would be here today. Because I believe, see them tough times taught me to find the God of my understanding. Now if I had never took that drink, I would never found AA. . . . A miracle happened when I took that drink. And a greater miracle happened when I found AA. Because if I hadn't went through them things

I don't believe I have that faith that I have today. Because today I know this. I can go through the storm, I can have peace through death. I can have peace through the storm. I can have peace when you lose one of your loved ones. I can have it today.

There was no trace of fear in Shirley's approach to death. As a matter of fact, that was the case for the majority of hospice patients we interviewed. There was almost no fear. Of course there was nervousness. Of course there was anxiety. But the people we spoke with weren't terrorized by the thought of death. The peace surrounding them was almost eerie at times. In the early interviews especially, when we were nervous about talking with dying people, we found that our interviewees were going out of their way to make us comfortable with the facts of their situation. *They* were putting *us* at ease!

It's one thing to slap a "No Fear" sticker on your truck when you are young and feel invincible. It's quite another thing to experience no fear when you are staring death in the face. Yet that's what we saw, over and over again. Denial isn't really an option for a hospice patient. There's no pretending you're going to live forever—at least not in this body. All you can do is face the fact that "it is appointed unto men once to die" (Heb. 9:27 KJV). We found that people who face that fact discover death has no power to frighten them anymore. And if you don't fear death, what else could you possibly fear?

The Bible makes it very clear that God doesn't mean for us to live in fear. When God speaks to people in the Bible— either directly or through an angel—the single most common utterance is: "Fear not."

- Fear not, Abram: I am thy shield and thy exceeding great reward. (Gen. 15:1 KJV)
- Fear not, for I am with thee, and will bless thee. (Gen. 26:24)
- Fear not to go down into Egypt, for I will there make of thee a great nation. (Gen. 46:3 KJV)
- Fear not, and do not tremble, neither be ye terrified because of them. (Deut. 20:3 KJV)
- Fear not, neither be thou dismayed. (Josh. 8:1 KJV)
- Fear not, Zacharias: for thy prayer is heard. (Luke 1:13 KJV)
- Fear not, Mary: for thou hast found favor with God. (Luke 1:30 KJV)

Consider what is happening in each of these instances: a human being stands before God Himself. The eternal has broken in on the temporal. Mortality stands face-to-face with immortality. That's an over-awing experience—an experience fraught with fearful possibilities. "The fear of the LORD is the beginning of wisdom" (Prov. 9:10). And yet that same God says, "Fear not." As the hymn "Amazing Grace" puts it, "'Twas grace that taught my heart to fear, and grace my fears relieved."[1]

The hospice patients we interviewed stood where Abram and Zacharias and Mary stood: at the meeting place of mortality and immortality, time and eternity. Most of them had heard—and heeded—God's words: "Fear not." Yes, it was hard. There was a lot of physical pain, a lot of emotional pain. But there wasn't a lot of fear. This wasn't mere stoicism or mental toughness. Rather, the peace and confidence that replaced fear came from the conviction that God loved them and gave them an eternal hope for the future.

Shirley expressed her faith as clearly as anyone when she said she didn't regret any of the horrible things that happened in her life. There at the end, God's love overwhelmed everything else for Shirley; all the hurt, harm, disappointment, despair, and anger were just swallowed up by the simple fact that God loved her and had a plan for her life. "Sometimes I believe death is a healing. I really believe that death is a healing."

Chapter 11

⌒⤜⋙⧓⋘⤛⌒

DEFEATING REGRET–
PROACTIVE DISCIPLINE

Carol had been a nurse—a hospice nurse, as a matter of fact—before she became a hospice patient herself. She helped a lot of people, and she was much loved by those who worked with her in clinical settings. Nevertheless, she experienced regret. "I didn't follow up on my wants," she said. "I wanted to be a nursing missionary. I just didn't follow through and I would have liked to have done that. Evidently, I didn't want it enough or I would have done it."

There was a time when Carol let herself make excuses. But now she understood they were just excuses. Now she understood what she missed out on. "Sometimes we use circumstances as an excuse. I think that's what I did. It was a cop-out. I didn't have to follow up. I could use excuses. And I did. I guess that's my loss."

Reflecting on Carol's regret is worthwhile for us all. Hers

was not a tragic regret, but her musings did create a strong sense of melancholy. What is the "take-home message" of Carol's story? I think she's telling us to follow our dreams, seize the day, go for it, just do it. Pick your cliché, but it's all about proactive discipline. Maybe that's the phrase: "proactive discipline." I can already see it in a sports drink ad. Being proactive—taking charge and moving forward with positive energy—but directing that action and energy with a stern will and with organized structure.

So many of the regrets our interviewees discussed had to do with being passive when they should have been assertive, hanging back when they should have been initiating. They didn't go to college. They didn't get out of a bad relationship. They didn't tell people how they felt. All because of inertia—because they let life happen to them instead of taking control of those things they were able to control.

If Carol's regrets were melancholy, the regrets of Rose R. rose to the level of tragedy. Not that she actually acknowledged her regrets. When we asked her if she had any regrets, she simply said, "Not anything important." We pushed her a little and asked if there were any unimportant regrets she could talk about. "I don't think so," she answered.

And yet her conversation was shot through with regret. Rose was eighty-three years old when we spoke with her. At the age of twenty she gave birth to a girl who was mentally handicapped. "It's been a struggle all her life," she said—that's sixty-three years she's talking about. "She just wallows away, can't do anything." Rose took care of her daughter alone; the daughter was forty years old before Rose ever got any help.

Don't misunderstand: Rose's tragedy wasn't the fact that she had a daughter who was mentally handicapped, or even that she devoted sixty-three years of her life to caring for her. The tragedy was the way Rose let that life challenge cast a shadow on everything about her life. We asked her about the most important thing she ever did. Here is her answer: "Not anything important. Tied down taking care of my daughter."

There's the tragedy in Rose's story. She didn't recognize the importance of taking care of her daughter, but instead felt that it prevented her from doing anything important. In any case, she let her life pass without really living it. That's a recipe for regret, even if she wasn't ready to admit to having any.

Regret, according to Merriam-Webster's online dictionary, is "sorrow aroused by circumstances beyond one's control or power to repair." To that definition I would add a qualification: the real point isn't the fact that regret-inducing circumstances are circumstances we can't repair. I can't bring rain to drought-stricken regions of the world; I'm sad about that, but I wouldn't say it's a personal regret because I have no power to affect the situation. The real point of regret is that there *was* a time when we could have repaired—or, better yet, prevented—the circumstances we regret, but that opportunity is gone. Rose couldn't change the fact she had a daughter who was handicapped. But her own attitude was in her power to control, and she chose not to.

One of the most interesting expressions of regret came from Susan. She told the story of a seemingly minor incident from probably forty or fifty years earlier:

> One of my sons was very allergic to bee stings. I looked around and [bees] were flying straight toward him. I ran to him to shoo the bees away, and they began to fly toward me! I panicked and ran from those bees. I lost my courage

and ran. . . . I'm so ashamed. He said, "Mom, you made those bees chase you." But I ran because I was scared.

There's a lot in that little story. The whole thing seems so minor: who hasn't run from bees? But Susan knew the issue was her heart, her character, and she was disappointed in the failure of courage that could have potentially caused dire trouble for her son. Never mind that everything worked out fine. Never mind her son gave her credit for being courageous rather than cowardly. Susan got a glimpse into her own heart, and she didn't like what she saw. That's a poignant aside: "I'm so ashamed." She's talking about something that happened decades earlier, something nobody would fault her for! Yet she still felt the shame of it. The shame of running away when she felt she should have stood firm. The shame of leaving someone she loved in the lurch.

In general people gave short responses to the question about regret. Some exchanges were productive, but many people simply refused to discuss their regrets. Judy's exchange with Lucille was pretty typical:

Judy: "Do you have any regrets?"
Lucille: "Oh yes. Too many to even think about."
Judy: "Is there any one thing that, if you could go back, you would do differently?"
Lucille: "Yea. I wouldn't do it at all." (Laugh)
Judy: (Laugh) "Can you tell me about that?"
Lucille: "No, I'm afraid I can't!"

When asked about regrets one woman responded, "I try not to think about those. I don't know that I have any. Of course, I wouldn't have my husband die, you know . . . not that I could control that." This is a good example of a disappointment rather than a regret. At some point we all face disappointments, and many of them are not in our control. What people seem to look back on with regret are outcomes they believe they could have influenced differently, but they didn't.

Almost every conversation revealed a regret of some sort. A few of them were heartbreaking, but most of them evoked more of a wistful mood. Our interviewees wondered about the "road not taken," speculated on "what might have been."

Given what we heard throughout our conversations, it shouldn't be surprising that people didn't talk much about their work life when they talked about their biggest regrets. There were a few. Theodore pointed to a time "when our company president—when we made a big mistake. But we had no way of knowing when he sold part of the company. I don't think there's anything I could have done. I would have done the same thing." As a university president, Emmit understated the politics of the academy when he said, "Some internal politics were kinda nasty and hardly worth, hardly worth keeping track of . . . ugly business." Those of us involved in university politics often say, "The politics are so intense because the stakes are so small." But they can cut deeper than we're willing to acknowledge. After all, Emmit mentions this as his only regret. Sam stated he probably stayed in one job too long. But that's about it. The conspicuous absence of work in our conversations is surely significant in our search for what really matters. That's not to say that work doesn't matter at all, but we do contend that work belongs in the second tier of what really matters.

The reader may be surprised to know that the most frequently mentioned specific regret in our discussions was related to educational attainment. Fifteen of our 104 interviewees said they regretted not getting more education. Willie F. said, "I might have gone to college longer, and got another degree, I only got my BS from Peabody in '32." Sam attained a master's degree, but still looked back with some regret when he said he was disappointed in "not getting to finish a PhD. I went back to school with a wife and two kids and I simply couldn't take care of my family and continue with school." In his case the regret was mitigated somewhat by the fact that his alma mater had awarded him an honorary doctorate in recognition of his life's accomplishments. In a display of his endearing humility he said, "I guess they ran out of names."

In the case of Reitha, the regret was an unfinished plan. "Well, only one thing that I can think of that I would do— get more education. See, I stayed home while my husband went to school and then he was gonna help out at home while I went to school . . . and it never did come my turn." Reitha was one of several people we talked to who just never got their turn to complete their education, having been thwarted by life's contingencies. Circumstances also prevented Chester from reaching his educational goals. His first regret "was that I couldn't go to college. My father passed away and (my mother) said, 'Forget it—we can't afford it.'"

Education lost seems to translate into opportunity lost for these folks. In the cases of several it was clear that educational attainment was linked to unrealized careers. "My biggest regret was not finishing law school," said Rodney, a contractor who specialized in building hospitals. "I always wanted to be a lawyer and I would have made [a good one]. I've been an expert witness in over a hundred cases . . . lawyers call me for advice and they send me contracts and say, 'Please read this and tell us how to change it so it will be fair to my client.'" But after this quick trip down the "road not taken," Rodney jumps back to the road he took and says, "But in a way I'm happy I deal with what I deal with in my life, because building hospitals is a great satisfaction because you're helping so many people."

As Christine looked back, she saw that her career advancement was somewhat limited by the lack of more nursing education. "I regret that I never went into nursing. I worked as a nursing assistant at different hospitals . . . and I found that I enjoyed it because I found that I could help people and I was able to meet them where they were and help them. It was a gift from God. It wasn't sympathy; I could empathize with them. I used to break all the rules. If I had to, I would climb in bed with them and hold them," she laughed, "but nobody said anything because that was all I could do!" Christine was a remarkable woman; we got the impression that her desire to be a nurse rather than a nursing assistant wasn't simply a matter of career advancement, but grew out of a desire to do more good for people. She did all she could do—even climbing in a hospital bed to hold a patient—but she regretted she couldn't do more. Education can do a lot of things for people, but what it can't do is create the kind of loving spirit Christine demonstrated!

Learning for Life

Carmen told us her greatest joy was learning something new. We're both educators, so we were gratified by her answer. But admit it: doesn't that answer surprise you a little? Don't you expect a woman on her deathbed to be beyond learning? When your lifespan is measured in weeks or months, isn't your mind supposed to be engaged in looking back at the past, or maybe looking forward to heaven? How are you going to "use" any new knowledge you might learn? The question itself—asking how one will "use" knowledge—reveals how utilitarian our approach to learning can be. But Carmen loved to learn because it made her feel larger on the inside.

Mary T. had a love for learning, too. She was learning a new sewing technique. She had always enjoyed sewing, and she wanted to master one more trick and make her granddaughter one more dress before she departed.

John B. was ninety-eight years old and had just weeks to live. Oh, and he was also learning Hungarian. He had always wanted to learn Hungarian. Also, there was a Hungarian-speaking woman in residence at the hospice facility, and he wanted to be able to talk with her in her native tongue. He might have said, "I'm ninety-eight. I'm at death's door. I guess I've missed my chance to learn Hungarian." Instead he said, "I'm ninety-eight. I'm at death's door. I'd better get busy, or I'll miss my chance to learn Hungarian!"

Regrets about marriage and other relationships came in at a very close second to regrets about education. They are treated separately in a later chapter. In those cases, too, the issue almost always came down to being passive where one should have been active—whether that meant not getting out of a bad relationship, not taking steps to heal a fractured relationship, or not communicating with loved ones.

We have talked about Thomas D. before, who left his sons behind with his former wife. "What I've done with my sons . . . it dwells on me, what I did. I could have been more, you know. I could've, I could've sent birthday cards on birthdays, I could've sent Christmas cards, but I didn't."

"Could've" but "didn't." There's the classic sentence structure of a regret. It seemed that when small regrets weren't confronted and reversed quickly, they built momentum, like a snowball rolling downhill. They just got harder and harder to confront. If you haven't talked to your child in a year, which is easier—wait another month or do it now? And after five years, it's really easier to wait than it is to take positive action. And as time moves on, eventually it is inevitable that one day, it's just too late.

The only point in mulling over the dying regrets of the soon-departed, of course, is to try to avoid similar regrets in our own lives. Our conversation with Harold M. is helpful in this regard. In eighty-four and a half years he accumulated very few regrets. Sometimes when our interviewees said they had no regrets, or few regrets, we frankly didn't believe them. It was obvious some of them simply didn't want to talk about their regrets. That was their right, but that's a very different thing from not having regrets. In Harold's case, however, it seemed pretty obvious he was telling the truth. "I think I've had a good life," he said, "as good as most people, and a long life and a great marriage I think. Nothing's perfect you know, I mean there's always little rumblings in there somewhere, but for the most part . . . "

"Don't Be Afraid to Try."

Fifteen years ago I was privileged to interview The Power of Positive Thinking *author Dr. Norman Vincent Peale and his wife, Ruth Stafford Peale, in their offices at the Foundation for Christian Living in Pauling, New York. At the time of this interview,* The Power of Positive Thinking[1] *had sold a million copies for every publisher that turned down the manuscript for this book—sixteen! Imagine that. Sixteen publishers told him his book was not worthy of publication, his ideas weren't important, he couldn't write well. And did he give up? The real story is he wanted to give up at times, but Ruth would not allow him to quit. She was his editor, motivator, and friend who said, "I believe in you." The result? One of the most important and successful books ever written has inspired millions of people to live a more meaningful life. I am convinced many people give up just before the victory. Several of the soon-departed were still seeking to complete the accomplishment of important goals in the final days of their lives as they encouraged us to "not give up!"*

In her own gentle way, Mary T. sent her own positive-thinking message when she said, "Don't worry about the little things. Enjoy all of it. And don't be afraid to try!" That's a great reminder. The only thing worse than giving up is never even trying at all!

Part of Harold's freedom from regret is the result of a balanced perspective and a positive attitude. We'll delve into that topic—not just Harold's great attitude, but that of several other of our interviewees—in the next chapter. For now, I'd like to look at something else Harold told us, because I think it's a real key to living a life with no regrets. "You've got to realize what's important," he said. "And the trivia of life, [you have to] set that aside to concentrate on things that are important."

There's Harold's recipe for regret-free living: think through what's really important in life, and take steps to make sure your day-to-day living reflects those priorities. "You've got to live life day by day, and make each day better if you can." We're always looking for a five-step program or a self-help book or maybe a grand gesture that will give us a new start and sweep away years of wrong-headed living. But as Harold points out, life—even a life that's eighty-four-and-a-half years long—comes at us one day at a time, one choice at a time.

A life with no regrets requires first that we know what really matters, and second that we make adjustments *every day* to ensure we're staying on course. Our environment, life's urgencies, even our own hearts conspire to throw us off course if we're passive, if we simply let life happen to us. The path of least resistance seems always to lead into the ditch eventually. As Harold said, we have to concentrate on the things that are truly important and set aside—actively set aside—life's trivialities. The irony, as Harold pointed out, is that sometimes the most important things in life *seem* trivial if you're not paying attention.

We all want to get to the end of life and look back without regret. Harold tells us how. Understand what is important and what is trivial—which may or may not be obvious at first glance. Then focus your energy accordingly. It's as easy as that. It's as hard as that.

The Tyranny of the Urgent

The "time management" concepts that emerged in the 1970s have proven to be beneficial to millions of people. They include methods that help prioritize activities, allocate time among activities, and enable a person to track results. One of the most memorable time-management concepts, "the tyranny of the urgent," was popularized by Alec Mackenzie in his 1972 book The Time Trap.[2] *This concept recognizes that so often we spend our precious time focused on doing urgent things. That makes sense until you think about whether "the urgent" and "the important" things in your life are the same. The simple but powerful suggestion of the time-management experts is to make a list of all of the things you feel are important in your life. Then make your to-do list for today and compare that list to what's important in your life. This comparison should then be used to prioritize your to-do list by ranking the most important and urgent items A, the second-most important items B, and the less-important items C. What is interesting to note is that Cs often contain urgent, but relatively unimportant items; however, unless one exercises strong self-discipline the Cs tend to get done first.*

"Urgent" is not the same as "important." We have the potential to live more meaningful and joyful lives if we can choose the correct "urgent" items and simply stop doing the others. This doesn't mean you don't have to file your taxes on time, but it could mean you decide not to respond to every promotional item that comes in the mail labeled "time sensitive." Once you begin to bring this sort of discipline to your personal time management you will find the truth in the oft-quoted phrase "If you can manage your time, you can manage your life." (It is frequently phrased "If

you control your time then you can control your life," but I know better than that.)

In the process of our interviews we heard from people who felt very good about how they aligned their time with their personal goals and what really matters in life. We also talked with several who would, if they could, spend their time differently. What we didn't hear from one single person is, "If I had it to do over I would spend more time at the office." We heard several regrets similar to that of James B. who told us, "I didn't spend enough time with my family, especially the boys as they were coming up." We need to listen. We need to hear those soon-departed. They know what they're talking about, especially when it comes to the ticking clock!

Chapter 12

DEFEATING REGRET– PERSPECTIVE

We talked about Harold M.'s advice to live intentionally: to decide what's really important and direct your energies that way. The idea is to avoid as many regrets and disappointments as possible through proactive discipline. But, as the old saying goes, "Into every life, a little rain must fall." Disappointments and regrets enter the happiest and best-lived of lives. And as we learned from many of our interviewees, managing those unhappy circumstances was a matter of perspective.

Harold said, "I've always felt like I've had a pretty good life, all in all." That "all in all" is key here. As we dug a little deeper, it became clear that Harold wasn't simply a golden boy for whom nothing had ever gone wrong. There were hurts and disappointments along his road. But he learned to see the big picture, and in the big picture, he could see that those things had a purpose, or at least they were balanced out by good things in his life. "If something went sour on me, it usually sweetened up a bit later on me, you know, leveled out. And I think that we all have points or little things that bother us, not going quite the way we'd like to see it, but I think if you wait long enough, they tend to level out somehow."

Harold was an architect and a painter, so it wasn't surprising to hear him continue with an artist's metaphor. "The way you picture this thing is going on, this little life, [is] a montage of life. . . . You can't pick at little things in a lifetime, I don't think. I think you've got to sum it all up, average it out, or whatever, and see what it comes to. And that's what I do, what I can do now is look back on things, little things that happened that I didn't particularly care for that in the long run seemed to work out okay."

"That's good to know," interjected Harold's daughter, who was sitting with us.

It really is good to know when you step back to look at the "montage of life," the overall vision of one's life doesn't have to be defined by regrets. To use another art metaphor, if you focus on one piece of broken tile in a mosaic, it's not very beautiful and doesn't appear to mean much. But when you take in the whole mosaic, it's astonishing to see what the artist has done with a pile of broken tiles. Think about those mosaics from the Roman baths—portraits, animals, landscapes—nothing more than broken tiles artfully arranged.

Our main hope in interviewing the soon-departed was to learn from them. To learn how to live life more fully and to learn what really matters. Our initial expectation was that we would hear a lot about what people would do differently if they had their lives to live again. As it turned out, we just didn't hear much of that. Sure, there were a lot of specific disappointing moments recalled, but so many of them were only recalled with prompting from us and people had simply not allowed disappointments to become regrets.

William S. was one of the most remarkable in this regard. William went into the ministry relatively late in life, after a career in the business world. He ended up in a tiny church in a sleepy little fishing village in Florida—a very long way from the lucrative sales career he left behind. "Have I had disappointments?" William said. "I don't think so. I don't think so. I think my life has been very rewarding. We've had lots of fun and we've had a few disappointments."

Then William remembered something he told us earlier in the conversation. He lost two children. One died in infancy. The other, a son, died at the age of nine in a sledding accident. They still had his picture on the wall. "The disappointment of losing two children, that's a terrible blow," William admitted. Then his wife reminded him of a business he once had that went bankrupt years before. "Yeah, we had a business we lost. I forgot all about that. But that was a long time ago. We didn't pine over it. That was fine. We got over it okay. We got over it okay. I think we've had a very good life and I'm not upset over this cancer business."

William S. never forgot the loss of his children. Nobody forgets that. But I was struck by the fact that he had to be reminded of his failed business. Imagine what a big deal it must have been at the time. You lose sleep when your business is failing; you feel humiliated, exposed; you're racked with fear about the future, unsure of how you're going to provide for yourself and your family. In other words, while you're going through it, losing a business feels like the kind of thing you could never forget, never get over. But when he was looking back on his life from his deathbed, it seemed like a little blip on the screen. It's worth noting that William's wife—who wasn't dying—did still remember that failure. Things look different from the front porch of eternity.

The soon-departed define success and failure differently from most of us. William was getting cards and letters from people whose lives he had touched. People he had known fifty or sixty years were coming to see him. Old parishioners drove from Florida to Tennessee to visit when they heard about his illness. "He's been very successful," his wife said. She was talking about his ministry in that little fishing village, where there were only eight hundred people in the whole town! By the world's definition, that's not what success looks like. But William and his wife weren't interested in the world's definitions. They were literally seeing the fruits of his labors.

"I think we've had a very good life." This from a man who experienced the death of two children, the bankruptcy of a business, and now a long, slow death from cancer. For many people that would be enough to cause them to declare their life as a miserable failure, but instead William called it "a very good life." How did he do it? His attitude was rooted deeply in his faith:

> The Lord has been so good to me, to us all our lives that we're ready to take whatever He brings us. . . . The Lord has taken care of us all the way. . . . And with this cancer business He's taken care of us. It's just beautiful and I'm not upset about it and I'm not mad about it. I'm very grateful for all that He has done for us and for all the people that have been so helpful and so wonderful to us, the hospice people and everybody else. We've had a really

great, wonderful life. I don't think we have anything to complain about. Do you?

William's words echoed those of Job from the Bible. After Job's friends had made long speeches—page after page in the biblical record—trying to explain his sufferings and giving him wrong-headed advice, Job finally managed to get a word in edgewise. His faith in God, he said, had nothing to do with his circumstances. "Though he slay me, yet will I hope in him," Job said. "Indeed, this will turn out for my deliverance" (Job 13:15–16 NIV).

But in my day-to-day struggles to achieve more and more, I often sound less like William and Job, and more like Joe Walsh. Remember that line from his song "Life's Been Good to Me So Far," where he complains even when there is no reason to do so? Why can't we see it? Why can't we see the blessings of our lives yesterday and today and celebrate those gifts rather than focus on what we don't have? An attitude of gratitude seems to be a certain path to discovering what really matters in life; remembering life is a gift and every gift should be accepted with gratitude to the One who thought enough of us to present us with the gift.

The "averaging" or "leveling" of life's events suggested by Harold was combined with the "attitude" of William S. in Donald's response. "There are always things you'd change. You can always be a better person. You can be a better Christian. You can be a better businessman. You can be a better father. You can be a better husband, you could be a better anything. But, when you boil it all down, when you look at it all, I've done about as good a job living as I could!" For Donald it really does "boil down" to doing your best, accepting your best as all you have to offer, and being at peace that your best is all that is expected.

These people get it. Julia S. said, "I've been blessed. I have no regrets. I've been bad; did some wrong. But I had a good life, kind parents and brothers. I can't complain." William M. continued the same theme when he told us he really didn't have any regrets and, in regard to his life, "It's just been so good that I can't complain about a thing." What a great feeling it must be: to reach the end of life and to not feel the need for any excuses and to claim to have no basis for complaining!

Most of the people we interviewed seemed satisfied with the lives they lived. They were pretty "to the point" when we asked what they regretted or what they would do differently:

- Jerry—"Nothing."
- Norma—"I can't think of regrets."
- Mickey—"No, not really."
- Lois—"No, none, no big things."
- Lawrence—"No, I think I'd do everything the same way."
- John B.—"I couldn't tell you anything really that I would do (differently)."
- Leon—"Well, I've been very happy with everything I've ever done."
- Mary H.—"I don't know that I would say that I do (have any regrets)."
- Carmen—"I don't think so."
- Charles D.—"I've had a good life. . . . I've never regretted any of it. I don't know that I would change anything. Like I said, I've had a good life!"

Money, Careers, Possessions

It was truly amazing how little "the 104" had to say about money and possessions and careers. You would think they'd slip up every now and then and say things like, "What gives me the most joy is my family . . . and my nice big house." Or, "I'm most proud of the work I did at the orphanage . . . and also the fact that I made partner at my law firm." But it just didn't happen.

Actually there were a couple of men who listed their business accomplishments and failures among their greatest joys and disappointments. But in the context of the other hundred or so interviewees, their remarks were so out of place as to be the exception that proved the rule. And, of course, there were several people who regretted having spent too much time working and not enough family time. A few men said they were proud of being able to provide well for their families. But the clear point there was family life, not work life. And one woman bragged about her son and daughter both making over $100,000 a year—but again, it was her kids she was bragging on; the money was just a vehicle for that.

Often when we were talking to the soon-departed, it was hard to believe these were people who spent decades putting in forty to fifty hours each week at a job—people who worried about money, had been greedy about money, spent hours and hours thinking about what to buy next or how to keep up with the Joneses. But surely they had. These were people we were talking to, not angels. Surely they had at one time been subject to the same weaknesses as the rest of us. But from where these people were sitting, none of that seemed to matter. It was almost beneath mention.

> Vicki put it colorfully: "You came in naked as a jaybird. You're going out naked as a jaybird." Here on earth we're judged every day by what kind of car we drive, what kind of house we live in, what clothes we wear. But the hospice patients we spoke with had already begun turning their attention to a much more important judgment. Harriet put it well: "It doesn't matter what kind of house, what kind of car, what kind of family, it's not going to matter who my daddy is. God's going to judge me."

We mentioned John G. in a previous chapter. His whole life was impacted by his developmental challenges, and he was dying of throat cancer. I asked him what he would change about his life and he said, "I wouldn't." As we experienced the love and care Maggie and Mike and the community were providing for John, we came to understand his satisfaction with his almost concluded life.

And perhaps Chester was the most clear and emphatic of all. When asked what he regretted about his life he said, "No. No regrets. No, no, no. Like I say, no regrets!" I got it. There were little things, but nothing that rose to the level of a regret. There really were numerous people who told us about some of their disappointments in life, but most stories were like those of Rodney and Lucille. They confessed they made mistakes and had disappointments, but they forgave themselves and tried to forget the disappointments and then moved on. One of the lessons that seems to be embedded in these stories is that bad things do happen, and they happen to everyone. And in the case of some really tragic experiences, you will never get over them. But you can move on beyond those experiences to find joy in life.

The emerging lesson seems to be if you want to be happy and feel good about the life you are living, why would you use time, energy, emotions, and brain capacity on life's disappointments? Why would you want to keep track of the nasty experiences? I think our soon-departed are once again onto something important about living life.

And Mary W. may have had the best response of all: "I don't really know. I don't have a problem with anything. I'm not changing anything. I'm living life just like I did before. I'm not going to worry about it!" That's what we all ought to be shooting for: living in such a way that we wouldn't change anything even if we knew we were about to die.

Benjamin said, "I hope to never regret anything. In everything there's positive and negative, happiness and sadness. I hope to find the goodness or positive in both." That search for "goodness or positive" in our entire experience was not lost on those who were in life-review mode and were looking at their lives as though they were hovering above it already.

Both Shirley and Harold G. suffered through some really tough times as alcoholics. And while both of them reported they regretted that others had been hurt along the way, they both specifically said they were glad for the tough times they endured. After going through Alcoholics Anonymous, Harold founded and ran a rehab center that helped many people. He believed his own experience was what made his treatment center so successful. He said,

> The alcoholism, it's one regret, to a degree—now I
> have to qualify this. I regret, my greatest regret is the ter-
> rible things that I did to my family, the terrible pain that

I caused them, and . . . the things I deprived them all of because I wasted the money on alcohol. These things are, you know, just devastating . . . I am not pleased with all the pain that I caused, but I am glad that I'm an alcoholic or I would not have found the program [Alcoholics Anonymous] to live by. So, I am glad I'm an alcoholic. Had it not been for this experience, there's no way I could have helped anybody else. My story is my greatest asset.

You probably remember Shirley, whose story was the basis for chapter 10. Shirley was raped at the age of eight, abandoned by her husband, and spent most of her teenage years and adult life mired in alcoholism. "I do not regret my past," Shirley said. I asked her to explain; it seemed to me she had plenty of reasons to regret or at least grieve over her past. Her answer was quoted in chapter 10, but I'm going to repeat it, because it demonstrates how the soon-departed are looking at the world through a different lens.

If I hadn't went through them tough times, I don't believe I would be here today. Because I believe, see them tough times taught me to find the God of my understanding. Now if I had never took that drink, I would never have found AA. . . . So, see that drink is, a miracle happened when I took that drink. And a greater miracle happened when I found AA. Because if I hadn't went through them things I don't believe I would have the faith that I have today. Because today I know this. I can go through the storm. I can have peace through the storm.

Vicki expressed a similar view when we asked about her regrets: "It's funny because there are several things I could say yes to, but the minute I say yes I'm going to totally destroy what effect has happened because of it." She told us how difficult her first marriage was, but then she went on to say, "I don't regret my first marriage 'cause I wouldn't have my two grandkids without it." And even though the marriage ended in divorce, Louise C. said, "No, I don't even regret marrying that man because he was wonderful, until the divorce. He was everything in the world to me. I don't have any regrets."

Like so many of our interviewees, Vicki now saw the big picture. That "montage" that Harold M. referenced at the beginning of this chapter has now come into focus for the soon-departed. They didn't all necessarily see it when they were going through it, but now they understand how it has all worked together to bring them to where they are today. And most of them were very satisfied with their lives and where they were. Imagine the difference in how you might feel about facing death if you had a sack full of regrets as compared to how you would feel if you could genuinely say, along with so many of the soon-departed, "I just don't have any regrets." Virginia told us how it feels to her. "I can't think of any big regrets. . . . I've given that a lot of thought, too, what should I have done differently. . . . I've thought all those things over and I've been a pretty, pretty decent person all my life. And it's a wonderful feeling, do you know that? I go to bed at night and I am so peaceful that I know that everything's been taken care of." Sweet dreams, Virginia.

Danger Zone

When we look back at the range of regrets people expressed, a few themes recur: mistakes in marriage, not achieving education-ally, tobacco use, alcohol abuse, drug abuse, not pursuing your dreams, and unhappy relationships. Is there a common denom-inator? One thing that many of "the 104" observed regarding these irretrievable mistakes is that they were still young when they made the initial decisions that led to these regrets. Many reported that they married too early in life. Decisions to drop out of school or to not continue educational pursuits are made by young people. And most people make decisions regarding drugs, tobacco, and alcohol as teenagers.

Those who study neurological development tell us the brain's development process is in a constant state of change throughout our lives; it is not really fully wired to the point we can describe it as "mature" until our early twenties. In the meantime, young people are choosing which road to take in life. The decade that covers the ages of thirteen to twenty-three can be described by poets or illusionists as "the wonder years," but may we suggest they are better described as "the danger zone" of life? These are critical years for making important decisions that determine what really matters in a life. What are we to do as parents, teachers, ministers? Hope to get lucky?

Praying would, in our opinion, be a better choice. But coupling our prayers with action is even better. Get involved and stay in-volved in the lives of young people. They need our love. They need our wisdom. They need our friendship. We can't abandon them to their friends. Except in rare cases, their friends don't know any more than they do, and, as most all of us were at their age, they are so self-focused they are rarely looking out for anyone but themselves. This may sound harsh, but reality does bite! We love young people. We've both given our entire lives educating a range of kids from eighth grade to graduate school. We've seen the very best side of young people who are able to navigate "the danger zone" and not only survive, but thrive; and we've seen it mean literal death to others.

Chapter 13

DEFEATING REGRET–
TREASURING RELATIONSHIPS

As has become obvious already, nothing means more to the soon-departed than relationships. Over and over again, we heard that people's greatest joy came from relationships, their proudest moments were when they loved well. It was relationships that gave purpose and meaning to their lives. On the flip side, it should come as no surprise that when our interviewees spoke of life's regrets and disappointments, again they had a great deal to say about relationships. We are relational beings. When relationships work as they ought, there's no greater happiness to be had on earth. When they don't, no amount of success or accomplishment can make up for it.

Of the 104 people we interviewed, a surprising fourteen said their biggest regret was having married the wrong person.

Fourteen! It was heartbreaking to hear the same story over and over again. One woman told of a marriage that made her miserable for seventeen years. It was passivity that kept her in the marriage, and it was passivity that made each day a misery. "I let him lead my life for me," she said. "He had affairs off and on, off and on, all along. I knew it, but he just had no respect for women at all. By the time that I got out of that marriage, I was drained. I bet I cried for three straight days. I was so happy to get out of it, but then I thought, *What have I got myself into?*"

Another woman described her regret when she said, "I should have left my husband earlier because there was just the suffering." After she left she "cried all night, but got up and went to work the next day." Janet told us her biggest regret was "marrying the guy I married the first time." However, like so many of the people we talked to, she refused to dwell on her regret. She declared, "But we won't go into that empty bucket!"

Another woman, when asked if she regretted anything, immediately said, "Yes. I really regret marrying someone that had been married before. Works out for a lot of people . . . " But it didn't work for her. "We just didn't have the same things in common. He didn't like the things that I did."

"He changed toward the last part of his life," she said. "You know, he told my brother before he died, when he was sick, that he wished that he had gone and done more things with me. But see, it was too late in life—too late. Of course, I don't mean to down him, but I guess that was the biggest mistake I ever made." One wonders why the man told his brother-in-law he wished he had treated his wife better, instead of telling it to his wife. It's that passivity, that unwillingness to take responsibility that leads to a cycle of regret, on both sides of the relationship. "Too late in life—too late." What a sad refrain to such a sad tune!

The male gender didn't come across very well in many of the stories we heard. At least one man was honest in laying out his greatest regret when he said, "I wouldn't have cheated that time if I could change anything. If I wanted to lie, I didn't have to tell you that." To be fair, however, gender was not a perfect predictor of "who done who wrong." Sometimes the women appeared to be playing the villain in the relationship. A couple of the men indicated that their greatest regret was related to their divorce experience, with one telling us that he just couldn't get over the fact his wife divorced him twelve years earlier after they had been married for twenty-six years. Several others mentioned that they had just gotten married too young, before they were ready for marriage.

Getting married was the biggest mistake and regret of some, but Richard A. came at this issue from another point of view. He described the "wild living that I went through in my teenage years and through my army years and up until my thirties or forties . . ." He thinks he started down the wrong path when he didn't marry. "Come to find out it was probably the worst mistake I've ever made in my life." But very interestingly, immediately after stating his deepest regret, unprompted, he celebrated his redeemed state. "I sound a little like a broken record about the Lord here, but I can't help it. The most important thing I think I've ever done was accept Him as my personal Savior. You know, I have eternal life now, and if I die or live it's okay."

We were a little surprised that so many people said they regretted their marriages and so few of them said they regretted they didn't try harder to save their marriages. But we weren't asking people to stick to our expectations; we were asking them to be honest. And they usually were.

The next-most common relationship regret we heard from "the 104" was not telling others how they really felt about them. Susan's only regret was, "I did not tell my husband enough how much I loved him, and I didn't thank him. He died two years ago and he gave his body to Vanderbilt. I don't have that kind of courage." Florence said, "I've had a lot of disappointments, but most of them were different ones of my family dying without me saying the things that I should have said to them. My sister, she died at forty-seven, and of course we knew it was coming—she had cancer—but you know, you keep putting off asking things you want to know." Florence's situation seemed especially regrettable: she knew her sister was dying, but she still didn't say or ask the things she knew she should have.

Lillie regretted "that I didn't show people that I loved them more." That realization was a direct result of her illness. As people gathered around, hugging her, expressing love to her, she regretted not doing that more herself during her life. "Hugs and stuff remind me that I was standoffish."

We heard the soon-departed talk about the common assumption that we'll always have more time. In the case of Calvin K., he said, "My mother was in her early eighties and I absolutely would not allow myself to think that she would ever die. . . . And I remember being with her when she was in the hospital one night and I began contemplating her death, then in an hour or two had to leave. Within two, three days, she died. And I did not have the kind of conversation that I would like to have had with her. A rather small thing, but it's symptomatic of how we do a lot of things. Always assuming that there will be a tomorrow, so we say, 'I'll see you later . . . ,' and sometimes that's not the case . . . and that's kind of sad." It's unavoidable: the day will come when "I'll see you later" simply isn't true.

The wife of Charles D. offered a simple solution to this easily avoidable regret: "I told everybody . . . ya'll keep forgetting to stop and tell everyone how much you love 'em, because you don't know if you're gonna have 'em tomorrow or not." She was quite a character on this point—quite insistent:

> That's something I'm really hard on—you leave this room, you walk out that door, I'm going to say that I love you, and I'm going to kiss you before you go out it. I don't care what you done. I don't care if I'm mad at you. You know, I've been mad enough at [my son] that I could just literally strangle him. I've thrown him off this property and told him, "If you set foot on here again, I'm going to shoot your butt." But at the same time, as he was leaving, I said, "You remember how much I love you, and you stay in touch!" I never knew love as a kid . . . I wasn't important to anybody. I never wanted my kids to ever have a day that they didn't know they were loved.

Vicki said, "I think my biggest disappointment would be, I wish my mother and I could've had a better relationship. I wish my mother and I could've had a relationship like my daughter and I have." Mildred, too, regretted not spending more time with her mother.

Children were another source of regret—occasionally because children didn't turn out the way their parents hoped they would, but more frequently because their parents re-alized mistakes they themselves made. Elsewhere we have discussed at length the monumental mistakes made by men who abandoned their children. But there were also plenty of people who were "there" for their children but now realized they weren't "there" enough.

Christine talked about time spent with her children.

I had four children close together. I wish I had spent more time with them when they were little. It was hard in those days. You didn't necessarily have automatic wash-ers and dryers. We didn't have dishwashers; we didn't go out to eat. If you wanted cookies, you made cookies, you baked bread, you had a garden, and you canned goods. That's the kind of thing you did. Well, in Wisconsin any-way.

It's a bad habit we parents have: "doing for" our children—or rather, "overdoing" for them—instead of simply being with them, which is what they really want. Lee knew all about it, and he regretted it:

The one thing I would change is not to work so much. Quit worrying about making more money, quit worrying about all the overtime I can make and spend more time with the family. I can't get over the fact that I wasted a lot of good time just so I could make more money for them. Family comes first, and I didn't realize that until I realized I'm dying.

Kathleen's regrets were similar to Christine's:

I pray a lot that the Lord will redeem my mistakes as a mother. Even though I only had one child, there were mistakes that I made that hurt her feelings or gave her a lower self-esteem—unintentionally, but those still can bring tears. [I regret] that I wasn't bright enough to know to hold back and that God would redeem it. That's my big, biggest disappointment.

The great news is that God *does* redeem the mistakes of mothers. One of the loveliest stories we heard was from Rodney. He was still a young man—only fifty-two years old—and his mother was still alive. She was never a very affectionate mother. "I lived fifty-two years and never once can I remember my mother saying she loved me," Rodney said. But his mother had sense enough to take advantage of her last chance to show her son how much she loved him. "Now when I speak to her," Rodney reported, "that's all she says—is how much she loves me so!" Her new willingness to be affectionate even extended to Rodney's wife, Dena; she began to call Dena her daughter for the first time. It may have been late, but it was not too late! A lifelong sorrow became a joy for Rodney.

As we said in chapter 11, regret is defined as "sorrow aroused by circumstances beyond one's control or power to repair." You may have made mistakes beyond your power to repair, but not as many as you think. In many cases it may not be too late to repair them. But the time will come when it *will* be too late. Those of us who are living and thriving—and especially young people—ought to listen to the voices of the soon-departed.

"It's Not Hurting Anyone but Me"

Some of the most common regrets voiced by "the 104" were related to addictions to tobacco, drugs, and alcohol. Sometimes the addictions were their own, sometimes it was their loved ones who were addicted. In a number of cases—especially lung cancers and emphysema for smokers—the addiction was directly related to the disease killing them.

Thomas D. was a smoker. He urged people not to make the same mistakes he did. "I started young . . . didn't listen to nobody and I thought I was it! [When it comes to smoking] don't even start. You have no idea what you're getting into. People told me, too, and I still smoked and totally disregarded their warnings." What does it take to get people to listen? Why do we disregard really good information and knowledge? The soon-departed have nothing to gain at this point, except the satisfaction that they spoke the truth, as best they knew it, with the desire to help others lead a life focused on what really matters.

Julia S. was straight to the point: "I wasted the best days . . . the best days in life. I spent it drinking and smoking. It's the worst thing in the world." Another woman said she regretted her drug use and "the time I missed with him [her husband]. I'll always regret." Her husband told us, "She's a loving person, a kind, kindhearted person. Always will go out of her way to help anybody. Anything that she has ever done has hurt her. She would never do anything to hurt anybody else. It [drug use] hurt the people that loved her but she didn't go out of her way to do it. It's just when you love somebody and they're hurting themselves, it hurts you too!" His wife said, "And I couldn't understand that because I tell myself . . . I'm not hurting nobody, but yes I was."

How many times do we see people hurting themselves, thinking that it's only about them, and pushing everyone away, especially those who really love them? What a powerful reminder that nobody is an island, even if we want to be. We say, "It's not hurting anybody but me," but we don't get to make that call. If someone loves us, it's their decision to love us. And if they are connected to us and we hurt ourselves, it will hurt them, too. And the closer the connection, the more intense the pain will be.

Chapter 14

FORGIVING AND BEING FORGIVEN

A few miles south of Little Rock, Arkansas, there is a small sign directed to the southbound lane of Interstate 30 that reads, "Prepare to Meet God." We've seen this sign hundreds of times over the past twenty-five years but are still sobered by the message.

Maybe the "hell-fire and damnation" preachers are not as far off track as many of us wish they were. While they can be criticized for leaning too heavily on guilt and fear at times, we should not miss the basic point—there will be a *Judgment Day* for each of us.

How does one "prepare to meet God"? And when does one "prepare to meet God"?

Almost all of "the 104" were preparing to meet God, and they were doing it as we spoke. People approaching death seem to realize that the grudges, the bitterness, and the anger at being hurt are a heavy burden they just don't want to take with them.

It's as if all of us go through life with a backpack attached. We begin life with an empty backpack. Over time we begin to load hurts and disappointments into our backpacks. Some of them heal and others we unload through forgiveness. But what we don't forgive begins to accumulate and get heavy. Eventually it seems life is missing some of the joy. You've seen old people who get grumpier and grumpier as they go along. Could it be because they're carrying around a backpack full of hard feelings toward people?

Imagine arriving in heaven, where your only hope of entering is God's grace and forgiveness. Then imagine God invites you to unload your backpack, and all you've brought with you is a load of complaints about people you've not forgiven. How would you explain that? Things could get pretty embarrassing pretty fast.

Most of the people we talked with were unpacking their backpacks of all the "unforgivens" as fast as they could. They didn't want to take them to heaven with them. Sometimes the contrast with the attitude of those around them was striking. We spoke with two sisters—one on her deathbed, the other tending to her—who lived terribly hard lives. They grew up together in orphanages, where they suffered physical and sexual abuse. They told many sad and horrible stories, but one episode that seemed to have hurt them most deeply was the time they were betrayed by their own mother. After years in the orphanages, they found their birth mother and went to see her. She agreed to see them, but when they got there, they were shocked when their mother told them not to tell anyone they were her daughters. She just told people they were company from out of town.

After telling this sad, sad story, the dying woman said, with a peculiar tenderness, "Of course, that's all right too . . . "

Her sister replied immediately and heatedly. "No! It's not all right!"

We had to agree with the sister. The things that happened to those two women were not all right. They were wrong, and nobody should have to live the way they lived. But that wasn't the point. That wasn't what the dying woman meant when she said, "That's all right." It was clear she simply meant she wasn't going to bear the burden of that anger and hurt to her grave.

The dying say, "It's all right." The living say, "It's not all right." It was a pattern we noticed more than once when there were relatives in the room. The irony is sometimes it was love and loyalty that made the living reluctant to forgive. They were unforgiving not of their own hurts, but of hurts suffered by their dying loved ones. They showed their love by refusing to forgive the same people their relatives had already forgiven.

Consider the case of Martha and Hannah. Martha beat breast cancer nine years earlier, but it was clear she wasn't going to beat lung cancer, now in a very advanced stage.

Her husband died a few years earlier, but Martha wasn't alone. Her grown daughter Hannah, the picture of filial piety, was always at her side, constantly tending to her every need. "I dress her up like a Barbie doll every day," Hannah laughed. She kept her mother's fingernails manicured, kept her jewelry in order.

It was the dutiful daughter, not the dying mother who sometimes cried over the finality of the situation they faced. It was mother Martha who offered comfort to the daughter:

" 'Whenever you feel like crying,' I told her, 'go ahead and cry.' "

They laughed a lot more than they cried, however. These two women clearly loved each other very much, and they were determined not to let Martha's terminal illness get them down for very long. They both spoke a lot about purpose. They were determined to find meaning in Martha's sufferings. Hannah spoke lovingly of the encouragement her mother gave to chemotherapy patients undergoing the same treatment she went through nine years earlier:

> When she was going through chemo she would be sitting in there getting that stuff that's making her sicker than a dog and she knows it was going to make her sick. But there was other women in there, like she went through the breast cancer, when she was going through the lung chemo while these other women were going through the breast cancer and they would be sitting there down in the dumps and I had Momma, you know, in spring colors and nothing dull and Momma would sit in there and talk to them and tell them, you know, don't give up. You know, I had that nine years ago and when you get that it will be over and done with.

Like so many of the people we interviewed for this book, Martha learned at the end of her life to live in the present. "I think that when your time gets ready for you to go, nobody can stop it," she said. "Until He gets ready for me I ain't going nowhere. If the Lord wants to call me home, that's fine. But until then . . . "

As the women began to talk about the past, however, a

darker undercurrent began to emerge. Martha mentioned that she cared for her husband for thirteen years after a major stroke. In fact, she said it was the most important thing she ever did. Thirteen years caring for an invalid would be exhausting in the best of circumstances, but Hannah shed some light on just how hard it was. "Daddy was not the perfect daddy," she said. "He was an alcoholic. When he got to drinking he tried to hurt Mom." He was also unfaithful. Worse, the other woman was Martha's sister-in-law.

It wasn't much later when Martha's husband had his stroke and he found himself depending on the faithfulness and kindness of the woman he had so wronged. Hannah had a somewhat gruesome view of the situation: "God took care of it in one way. [Daddy] couldn't abuse her. He couldn't go out on her no more."

Martha found herself in a position to take revenge on an abusive, unfaithful husband. But instead she forgave. Hannah marveled at her mother's forgiving spirit. "She still stood by his side and took care of him until he died and she never looked back. She [even] forgave the person, the sister-in-law she caught him with."

"I forgave both of them," said Martha. "I didn't want no hard feelings."

It was Hannah, not her mother, who harbored hard feelings as a result of her father's affair. "I have a lot of anger," she admitted. "I still have a lot of anger that the woman who slept with my father is still in the family."

There are a number of factors that help explain these two women's very different view of forgiveness. Martha may have simply had a more forgiving temperament than Hannah. But the most important factor seemed to be this: Martha no longer had the strength to hold grudges. Hannah was a strong and energetic woman. But Martha's life was ebbing away, and she refused to waste any of it on bitterness. She seemed to have made a conscious decision to devote her remaining energies to loving and reconciling. She spent the last of her life force on that which builds up and affirms life, not that which tears it down.

The soon-departed have it right. If it's a good idea for them to forgive and let go of old hurts, it's a good idea for us to do it, too.

Letting go was what finally made it possible for Shirley to get on with her life. She told us that in the entire time she lived at home with her mother and father, she could never recall her father making a kind or encouraging statement to her. She said he almost never said anything at all to any of the twelve children in the house. They were together with him every day, but the relational distance between them was enormous. Robert Bolton once wrote, "Proximity without intimacy is inevitably destructive [to relationships]."[1] In other words, being around someone routinely and not interacting with them at all, or in a superficial manner, sends the message *I don't care about you.*

In the case of Shirley, the message was received loud and clear and she harbored great resentment toward her father. When asked her greatest disappointment in life she responded: "Not being loved. . . . Never had a conversation [with my father]. . . . My father never sat down and talked like we're talking . . . and I resented that. Even though he was dead, I resented it because I felt like he had robbed me. . . . He robbed me of my childhood. And I kept that with me a long time . . . for so many years."

Eventually, however, after Shirley got into therapy, she found a way to forgive. "[Now] I bury it. I forgave my father and I bury it. Because I went back. I know my therapist told me to write him a letter and tell him exactly what I had to tell him . . . and I did that. Down in that letter I began to weep. Because I didn't realize how my grandparents had raised him. He only did what he knowed . . . and I forgave him and therefore developed peace." It's an amazing story. Shirley broke through her own resentment and tried thinking about what life might have been like for her father. He put an enormous distance between them, made it almost impossible for young Shirley to think of him as a human being with feelings and fears and hopes. But Shirley crossed the chasm. And even if it was too late to connect with her father, Shirley felt real healing and real connection. "If I could have went to the graveyard and called my father out and put my arms around him and told him I loved him, I would have did it. I would have did it. Because I remember praying that I would wish he died. How could he treat me like that? I realized that I prayed the wrong prayer. I could pray that God make him a better father."

Forgiveness is not a natural response to being wronged. Actually forgiving someone for a serious hurt is one of the most difficult things we can ever do. The most natural response to being wronged is the one Graham Greene articulates in his 1948 novel *The Heart of the Matter*: "Revenge was good for the character: out of revenge grew forgiveness."[2] In today's vernacular we would say something like, "I don't get mad, I get even!" And after all, a wrong demands justice—right?

Forgiveness is at the very core of the Christian faith. It is God's gracious, forgiving nature that enables people to have a relationship with Him. And that ought to translate into a willingness to forgive. Remember Jesus' story about the unforgiving servant? A servant owed the king more than he could possibly pay in several lifetimes, so the king began taking steps to sell the servant and his family into slavery. The servant threw himself on the king's mercy, and the king—surprisingly—forgave the huge debt.

It wasn't very long, however, before this forgiven servant went to collect a debt owed to him by another servant. The debtor threw himself at the forgiven servant's feet and begged for mercy, just as the servant did before the king. The debt was the equivalent of a few hundred dollars—the tiniest fraction of what he himself had been forgiven—and yet the man was adamant that he had to be paid immediately. He grabbed his debtor by the throat and choked him. He then had him thrown into debtor's prison.

The other servants witnessed the whole thing and went to tell the king about it. The king, as you might imagine, was furious. Jesus' conclusion to the story is sobering: "In anger his master turned him over to the jailers to be tortured, until he should pay back all he owed" (Matt. 18:34 NIV). God forgives us huge debts—debts we could never begin to pay, even if we lived several lifetimes. Why, then, do we find it so hard to forgive the paltry debts owed to us?

One good way to cultivate a forgiving spirit is to get in the habit of asking forgiveness. Asking for forgiveness is an ultimate act of humility. It's not only admitting you were wrong, it's giving up control and handing the authority to another person to decide what they're going to do with your humility.

If you're having a really hard time forgiving someone, then perhaps it's time to pull out a mirror and spend some time contemplating some of the hurts you've caused. If you can't think of any, congratulations. But if you can, then the righteous throne you sit on to judge and condemn others collapses, and forgiving others becomes more tolerable.

Another issue is self-forgiveness. We talked to many people who had some major regrets—so many we have devoted a couple of chapters to them. Those people were at various stages in forgiving themselves and dealing with the hurts they inflicted on others and even on themselves. William E. was the person who seemed to be having the hardest time forgiving himself for his mistakes. It was obvious he had a lot of good qualities, but he seemed unable to see them himself. His backpack was still pretty heavy with times when he had not forgiven himself. It was hard for us, seeing such a good man struggle unnecessarily.

William E. seemed convinced he had ruined his life with bad choices—convinced he never could get it right. When we asked what he regretted, he answered,

> My choices. Choices I've made. The ignorance I went into things with, thinking that, that I knew way more and making the wrong choices in probably ninety-nine percent of them. Being ignorant and thinking that you know and you don't know nothing. Just completely screwing up your life, and those with you in certain circumstances and everything else. Making an ass out of yourself.

William's regrets were so deep he told us he was having a hard time forgiving himself, so he didn't know if he should even ask God to forgive him. It was tragic. We are able to forgive ourselves—just as we are able to forgive others—because God has already forgiven us. William had it backward; he thought he had to come around to self-forgiveness before he could seek God's forgiveness.

You may or may not have made mistakes as dramatic and damaging as we heard about in our interviews, but all of us have made some pretty serious blunders. To achieve genuine peace and contentment in life you must be able to forgive yourself, and not just for you, but for the people around you. If God forgives you—and He does—by what authority can you refuse to forgive yourself? When we constantly engage in self-recrimination, we make life harder for everyone around us. As a management and economics professor I taught a course called Organizational Behavior for many years. Organizational Behavior attempts to understand human behavior at work. The discipline has its roots in psychology and sociology. Sometime around 1980 I first ran across the concept of forgiveness as a chapter in the textbook we used for the course. Today, forgiveness has become a cornerstone concept in psychology, counseling, and management-behavioral theory.

When you stop and think about it, genuine forgiveness for a serious wrong seems pretty rare. Check your own file—how many people do you have on the unforgiven list? It's easy to pile up a pretty long list, even one including numerous petty offenses. The emotional burden of carrying around a backpack full of unforgiven issues can get really heavy.

It's a burden the soon-departed weren't usually willing to carry. You might consider unloading your backpack now, while you've still got plenty of options for using that saved emotional energy.

Chapter 15

HOPING FOR HEAVEN

Kenneth must have felt a little like George Bailey from *It's a Wonderful Life*. He was one of those unusual people who get the chance to look back over their lives and see the impact they've made on the lives of the people around them. He invested his life in his community: his church, Boy Scouts, the high school band. And here at the end of his life, all the people he blessed were coming back and blessing him. His struggle with ALS (Lou Gehrig's disease) was difficult—no question about that—but its lingering effects made it possible for Kenneth to see his good deeds come back to him. In his friends' service to him, he was allowed to see what he meant to them.

We spoke to Kenneth at the end of October, and he told us somebody at church brought him lunch every day since the middle of the previous December. That's ten and a half months of meals! His life obviously meant a great deal to a lot of people.

Kenneth's brother came from out of town to visit him and was surprised to see Kenneth's great attitude. "He asked me how I was handling this death warrant so well. I told him, 'It's real easy when you let eight hundred of your closest friends take control. Because there's eight hundred of them down there [at the church]. They bring lunches, they pray, they mow the grass, they fix stuff—whatever's needed. And all we have to do is ask. Sometimes we don't even ask. We are very blessed."

But as important as his friends' kindness was, the real key to Kenneth's great, thankful attitude lay elsewhere. The defining desire of Kenneth's life when we met him was the hope of heaven. "Well, hey, I don't have my long-term life in order, so my long-term goals are to die and go to heaven. The sooner the better."

There's an old hymn—

Turn your eyes upon Jesus.
Look full in his wonderful face,
And the things of earth will grow strangely dim
In the light of his glory and grace.[1]

That's where Kenneth was: the things of earth were strangely dim as the prospect of glory came closer and closer. "Years ago," he said, "I would have said, 'Well, I've got other stuff to do. I'm ready to go, but I'm not willing.' Now I'm willing. . . . The hope of heaven is making my life, my death coming a lot easier."

Kenneth observed the difference in people who shared his physical condition but didn't share his hope of heaven. "In the ALS community, there have been a couple of folks with no religious affiliation—nothing. They're the ones that are bitter. They're the ones that fight for the last breath. 'Try this on me. Experiment on me. Keep me alive . . . ' Let me go. I'm ready, and it won't be long."

For Gary, it was the hope of heaven that gave him confidence he was where he needed to be. "I know where I'm at right now—here is where I need to be at. I mean, I'm close to seeing glory!" Gary experienced a complete turnaround in his life. He went from living completely for himself (and making himself and others miserable in the process) to living for God and others. He discovered in the process that fullness of life was in giving himself away. Gary's miserable life—punctuated by prison terms, broken relationships, and homelessness—had been transformed into a life of purpose and joy. It seemed a cruel trick that he should be struck down with terminal cancer so soon after he got his life in order. But Gary didn't view it that way. He viewed his new life as a foretaste of heaven—a foretaste that made him all the more eager to experience heaven in its fullness. "I'm close to seeing glory." He was moving from glory unto glory—from a good life to the best of all lives.

Many of us talk about heaven. But it was obvious the people we interviewed were making the transition. William S. spoke of his union with God the Father with a childlike intimacy: "What comes next? To see my Daddy. My big Daddy. My heavenly Father." Richard A. admitted he was getting a little "antsy" about the unknowns as the end approached, but ultimately his nervousness was swallowed up by the hope of heaven: "When I take my last breath . . . that's when I'll be in the presence of the Lord and I know that's where I'll be. Whatever comes to get me will come and get me, and I'll go on, and I'll be fine, you know. So that's the way I look at it."

A small group of our interviewees didn't look at things that way; they either didn't believe in heaven or were unsure. Calvin K., a Unitarian minister, said he wished he could believe he would soon be in heaven, but he just couldn't.

> If I had any idea that I could be with my extended family again, that would be as exciting as it could be. I could even say I would wish that were true. But my intellect would never allow me to say it will be true. I don't think it is. I don't push that on other people. I guess some people just can't deal with the frustration, the question of death, without leaving some room for other possibilities. And it would be cruel if I were to talk those people out of believing that way. I don't ever do that. But I will say if I concentrate on the quality of this life, things that I can do to make my life worthwhile in this life, there's nothing a heavenly promise could ever match what's right here. What's beautiful—flowers, trees, mountains, rivers, it's all here. I think that we've got to accept that this is it. And it's all of it. And if we thought this is all there is, then we would treat it a lot better than we do. We would look and see and appreciate more than we do. So the concept of life you're after [in this book], I think it's an unfortunate waste because it undermines the quality in this life. Does that make sense?

We agree we should concentrate more on the quality of *this* life, appreciate the beauty of *this* creation more, and treat the earth with more respect. But do we have to give up a heavenly promise to do that?

Our best estimate is that about 100 of our 104 interviewees harbored hopes of heaven. People have lots of different opinions regarding the words and the phrases we should use to express the transition from life to life, but they mostly agreed on the destination—heaven. Maxine said, "I don't use the words "passed away." My husband didn't pass anywhere, he died. I didn't lose him, he's not lost. I know where he is—he's in heaven, probably playing golf!"

Harold M. wasn't totally sure of how exclusive heaven would be, but in the latter part of his eighty-four years he began to be more open to the possibilities: "Somewhere there's a heaven and all the good people, presumably for the ones that are Christians only." Here he paused, not sure what he thought about that idea of exclusivity. "I sometimes wonder about that." William M. was similarly humble and less dogmatic when he talked about heaven. "Somebody's going to heaven. I don't doubt that at all," he said. "I'm just trying to live in such a way that when I'm done with this . . . I want to make sure I'm on the right side of that."

When asked, "What comes next for you?" Willie F., age ninety-four, sounded a bit mysterious at first. "I don't know. The wind I guess. It just blows me the way it wants to." But she went on to clarify the mystery: "It's still Jesus." William S. said, "The Lord's been good to me and I will pass on and be with Him in His heavenly kingdom. I'm looking forward to it!" And Rose D. had a clear focus and prayer: "I hope it's heaven. I hope it's heaven. I pray that it's heaven!"

People have sought a "promise of heaven" since the beginning of time. As we talked with Donald we heard that he received and accepted such a promise. "The only thing that is promised is, if you're a spiritual person, is that you have an opportunity to go on. There's no perfect promises here on earth, but all you have here is this promise: . . . if you take the faith and use the faith opportunity, then there's an opportunity for a better life. . . . That promise is original, and I'm going to take advantage of that promise." Christine had also claimed the same promise. "My thing now is to die with dignity and to go to heaven and see Jesus and look at the devil and say, 'You never could shut me up!'"

Some Attempts to Beat Death

When the universe was set in motion and humans created, the whole system was endowed with a set of laws to govern its operation. Some are laws of physics—time, space, and motion. Some are laws related to the nature of matter and chemistry. Others are spiritual laws that exist whether we understand them or not. Others are biological and physiological laws related to the existence of life. One of these biological laws is everyone has to die.

The intrigue and interest in finding a way to live forever, or to at least find a way around death, is at least as old as recorded history. The practices surrounding death utilized by the ancient Egyptians suggest a strong desire to live forever. Spanish explorers and others were motivated to endure great hardship and risk death in search of "The Fountain of Youth."

More recently the controversy surrounding the fate of the body of deceased baseball great Ted Williams divided a family, not to mention it also divided Ted Williams's head from the rest of his body. One daughter sought to have the body cremated while an-

other daughter and son insisted they made a pact with their father that the three of them would use cryogenics to be reunited in life in the future. The son and daughter won the day and his head was separated and frozen in a can of liquid nitrogen while the remainder of his body is stored upright in a larger container of liquid nitrogen. The hope of course is that future advances in medical science will be able to bring Williams back to life. It is estimated that a few hundred others have followed the same route in their aspirations for immortality.

"The Man Who Would Murder Death" is the title of an October 28, 2005, article by Thomas Bartlett in The Chronicle of Higher Education. The article reports the work of "rogue researcher" Aubrey de Grey, who is challenging the scientific world to halt, or even reverse, the impact of aging. Dr. de Grey believes some people living today could live a thousand years if science is able to solve some very fundamental, basic biological issues—like how to deal with damaged or lost cells. His science seems extreme, but Dr. de Grey's theory is attracting interest from some highly regarded, mainstream researchers. For example, the article reports that at a recent conference sponsored by Dr. de Grey, a Wake Forest University researcher showed slides of human organs that had never been inside a human, but had been grown from a few healthy cells taken from the person.

Is it possible that with all of this effort we might be able to overcome basic biological and physiological laws? Not likely. Not even Dr. de Grey is suggesting a person can live forever. And even if we could, there still remains the question, who would want to live forever in this body? The Bible has several things to say about the inevitability of death, but the message is succinctly summarized in Hebrews 9:27 with these words: "It is appointed for men to die once and after this comes judgment."

Sam was a college professor and, later, a college treasurer/ CFO. We asked him where he got the courage to face death. He spoke of expectant joy:

> I really don't discuss this too much—maybe I ought to discuss it more. It's probably my religious faith to be honest about it. I know where I'm going and I know where my wife is going. I know where my parents went and where my in-laws went, and I'm looking forward to seeing them again, every one of them. . . . The last adventure that I know is leaving this world and going to another one.

Sam talked about the fact that not only he would be going to heaven, but his wife would be, too, and that his in-laws and parents were there already. That was a very common theme as our interviewees talked about heaven—they took joy and confidence from the belief they would be reunited with loved ones who had gone before. It was a source of comfort for not only the dying, but also those who loved them. Mildred told a very sweet story: "My son Randall started crying before he left here. I said, 'Don't cry. You just go ahead and live you a good life, and if I don't get to see you again here, we'll meet up in heaven with Mom and Dad and the rest of them.' And he quit crying right then." She was headed for a place where there will be no good-byes—just one long hello. There God "will wipe every tear from their eyes. There will be no more death or mourning or crying or pain, for the old order of things has passed away" (Rev. 21:4 NIV). Not only was Mildred confident she would get there; she was confident her son would catch up with her eventually.

Norma got it exactly right. She longed for heaven, but in the meantime she intended to serve others as much as possible.

> Right now . . . I'm getting strength and going back to [my son's] house, but then I'm ready to go to heaven. You know, if the Lord can use me, I would like to be able to read to people who can't see, help bathe people who can't bathe, all the things that have been done for me since I have had cancer. I would like to voluntarily help people do that. I didn't know there were so many good people. That's what I'd really like to do, but if He wants me to come on home in the next few minutes, I am sure grown up enough to do that! Really, that's the best place—home is up there. Either way, I'm going home!

Norma just wanted to go home. Home to her son's house would be wonderful—more time with her family, more opportunities to serve and love others. But Norma knew she would never truly be home until she got to heaven. She sounded like Paul: "If I am to go on living in the body, this will mean fruitful labor for me. Yet what shall I choose? I do not know! I am torn between the two: I desire to depart and be with Christ, which is better by far; but it is more necessary for you that I remain in the body" (Phil. 1:22–24 NIV).

There's a reason we sometimes feel so ill at ease in this world. It's because this isn't what we were made for—not ultimately, anyway. We were made for heaven, and we'll always be a little restless until we get there. The more we talked to the soon-departed, the more we realized how many of them understood in their bones what we, the healthy and thriving, usually understand only in the abstract: death is only a transition from life to life.

In his novel *Godric*, Frederick Buechner puts it this way: "All the death that there ever was, set next to life, would scarcely fill a cup."[2]

That's the promise of heaven: you look around this world, and death seems like the most final, unavoidable fact of existence. Everybody dies. True enough. But when our thoughts turn to heaven, we see the big picture: death is puny compared to the vastness of life.

Regarding Hell

We heard a lot of talk about heaven from the soon-departed. Hell was rarely mentioned, perhaps because almost everyone we talked with had a hope for heaven. Hell is a very unpopular topic of conversation, debate, and even sermons, as today's most popular preachers focus on all the "feel good" subjects. In our self-focused world, hell is often considered a topic that just gets us off track. And, let's face it, we don't want to talk about it either—eternal suffering and separation from God and all that goes with that?

In 2003 the Harris Poll organization conducted a survey asking people a variety of questions regarding their religious beliefs, including: "Do you believe there is a hell?" The responses revealed that 69 percent of the American population believe in the existence of hell, but only 1 percent believes they will go to hell when they die. By contrast, 82 percent believe there is a heaven and 63 percent believe they will end up there.[3]

An authoritative word on hell can be found several places in the Bible, but none clearer than the words spoken by Jesus in Matthew 25:41 as He addresses those who refused to provide food or drink for those in need, refused hospitality to strangers, refused clothes to those in need, and didn't visit the sick or those in prison. Jesus said, "Away with you, you cursed ones, into the eternal fire prepared for the Devil and his demons" (NLT). Those are some pretty tough words, and we should carefully consider what they mean for the way we live our lives.

Do you think hell is real? It's a question worth thinking through and finding a definitive answer. Because at the end of life, it won't matter "what you think is the truth"—what will count is "what is the truth." This will be an answer that really does matter!

Chapter 16

THE FINAL HEALING

It was one of those stories that catch you totally off guard, driving the point much deeper into your soul, because you just didn't see it coming. Brenda Harris stood before our church congregation and told us about her daughter Amber. Amber's life seemed like the dream come true we all wish for our children. Having recently graduated from college, she was married to her high school sweetheart and was looking for that first teaching job. But along the way, she just couldn't seem to rid herself of persistent flu-like symptoms. One blood test later, her whole world changed. It was one of the most dreaded outcomes possible: leukemia. With the help of wonderful nurses, doctors, and a first-rate cancer treatment center, she battled hard through a round of very aggressive chemotherapy. After two months in the hospital, hope returned; the leukemia went into remission and Amber was able to go home in June.

After spending a great summer with her husband and family, Amber was able to begin her dream job—teaching the sixth grade at the same school she once attended. Her dreams were again interrupted just a few weeks into the school year as the cancer returned. The doctors and health professionals responded aggressively with a treatment regimen of chemo and a bone marrow transplant that was designed to at least send the terrible disease into remission, if not vanquish it forever. This hope was followed by more bad news. Despite the very best medical treatment available, the leukemia remained. Brenda said, "The doctors wept as they told us they had done all they could."

Amber went home and began to live as much as possible in those final days. I didn't know the Harris family personally, but I, like the rest of the congregation, was very emotionally invested as Brenda told the story. So I felt a shock of joy when Brenda said, "And then God miraculously healed her . . ." but the joy was mixed with confusion when Brenda finished her sentence ". . . and took her home to be with Him."

"God miraculously healed her . . . and took her home to be with Him." This story communicates better than we could ever explain what we mean by "the final healing." Here's a mother—and make no mistake about it, she is a broken-hearted mother who has seen her beloved child taken from her at an early age—who still has a genuine sense of peace regarding her loss. Amber was miraculously healed.

The attitude that "death is the final healing" was widespread among those we talked with in the Alive Hospice program. Some even used the same words. Shirley, dying after a prolonged struggle with breast cancer, said, "Sometimes I believe that death is a healing. I really believe that death is a healing!"

Maddie's mom, Jennifer, expressed great appreciation for all the extraordinary work the doctors, nurses, hospice workers, and entire health care system did for this five-year-old, but when their efforts of healing no longer mattered, she seemed to long for the final healing: "Maddie's been in so much pain and she can't make it through the day without strong, strong narcotics. Some days she just crawls because it hurts too bad to stand and bear the weight on her spine. The headaches are unbearable. I would prefer at this stage, after watching it for so long, to let go and have Maddie pass and be in heaven where she's whole, healed, and pain free."

She went on to say, "I'm not afraid for Maddie. I know that Maddie will be okay. The ones that will have to suffer the loss will be us. I will miss her every day. I don't know how I will bear it without her." Only a mother or father, or brother or sister, or husband or wife, or close friend of someone who has endured the worst of what this world has to offer could understand the contradiction. "I don't know how I will bear it without her" on one hand and "I would prefer . . . to let go and have Maddie pass and be in heaven where she's whole, healed, and pain free." This is genuine, true, sacrificial love that comes from a deep and rich faith.

When we experience or hear stories of tragic loss it's not unusual for us to ask God, "Why does this happen?" After all, we call it *tragic* because it violates our own world-shaped view of what is fair or just. The *why* question in this context is well captured in Rabbi Harold Kushner's terrific book *When Bad Things Happen to Good People*: Given that God is all-powerful, just, loving, and righteous, why do bad things happen to good people, and equally troubling, why do good things happen to bad people?[1] But Kushner's title is *When Bad Things Happen to Good People*, not *Why*.

Why is a whole separate book, or several of them. But our interviews did yield some interesting observations. Maxine dove right into the deep end on this theological question. She said, "My biggest disappointment was the fact that my husband died at the age of fifty-one—he was only fifty-one! You know, a lot of people get angry with God and . . . look up and say, 'Why me?' But I've always felt He will look down and say, 'Why not?'" Through the experience of interviewing and then writing this book, we've been struck with numerous profound insights, but none more compelling than this. Why not ask "Why?" How would you answer if God asked you "Why not?" What would you say? How would you build your case?

Maxine continued:

> I think God is just as upset over accidents and murders as we are. I think that He is just as upset. A lot of people believe everything [that happens], He does. I don't think God should get a bad rap, because He's not responsible [for all the bad things]. He created the world and He created the people in it. He didn't say . . . that we're not going to have evil—He didn't say that. He didn't say that we're not going to have stumbling blocks and things to struggle with—He didn't say that. Nowhere in the Bible does it say that you are not going to have struggle and sorrows.

What God did say, over and over and over, is He understands our sorrow and pain, He will love us through it, and He is with us. Shirley understood it. She was in counseling to help her cope with the fact that she was leaving her children and family behind. But one day the counselor came to Shirley with a problem. Like me, she clearly recognized the deep wisdom Shirley possessed, so she turned the tables. The counselor's nephew was the driver of a car in an accident. While all four passengers in the car were killed, her nephew survived. He came to his aunt, the counselor, and asked, "Where was God, where was God when my friends were dying?" She asked Shirley how to answer such a question. Shirley had a ready answer: "God ain't moved! He at the same place where His Son hung on the cross for us. He at the same place!" Through His life and death, Jesus earned the title of "Suffering Messiah." Emmanuel, the God who is with us, suffered in every way we suffer.

Whether it's Rabbi Kushner's Jewish perspective or John Claypool's Christian perspective from *Tracks of a Fellow Struggler*,[2] the same basic belief is key: God is with us. And God's very presence is healing. And the fullest healing comes when at last we are fully present with God.

"How Do You Measure the Value of a Life?"

Without question, the most difficult situation we encounter in our leadership roles at our university is confronting the mortality of our students. We are never prepared for the loss of vibrant, smart, energetic young people whose potential seems limitless. I write this just three days after the tragic rampage on the campus of Virginia Tech that took thirty-three lives and left all of us stunned and confused. It takes a lot to get the attention of our society these days, but this event certainly did get our attention. And hopefully it will keep our attention long enough for us to come to understand what happened and what our response should be to this event. It will be important that we not just write off this event as the act of one deeply disturbed individual and hope for a better day as we move forward. The very sad truth is there are multiple tragedies occurring every day that leave us shaking our heads and wondering what went wrong.

On those rare but still too frequent occasions when we find ourselves addressing parents and friends of students who have gone on ahead of us, we struggle to understand. We struggle even more to express our thoughts and emotions. We want—we need—to know that the life of the one we loved mattered, made a difference. How do you measure the value of a life?

This is a really difficult question. We talked with people whose time on this earth ranged from 5 years to 16 years to 42 years to 94 years to 102 years. One thing was clear: you don't measure the value of a life in terms of time spent on earth. What, then, is the measure? Most often the answer comes in terms of what the person has accomplished or what one has been able to acquire and accumulate in life. You've seen the bumper sticker: "He Who Dies with the Most Toys Wins!" It doesn't take much thought to find the emptiness and futility in that belief.

Here's what we heard from the soon-departed: the measure of a life lies in what we have been able to give to other people. At the memorial service for one of our students we were reminded that Lauren was a giver. She gave her time in community service. She gave her energy to everyone she encountered. One Christmas when she was in high school she asked her parents to do something different. Rather than purchase gifts for her, she asked them to buy books for a library she established for kids. She gave love to everyone around her. Lauren gave herself away. Vince Gill and Al Anderson expressed it well in the wonderful song "What

You Give Away." The soon-departed comprehended the full depth of this profound truth that giving is better than taking. They knew what they were taking with them as they departed, and it was something you aren't able to see, touch, or hear. But it was surely something they could feel in their hearts. It was the love they gave away that was the measure of their lives!

Both Lee and William E. struggled with the idea of incapacity. Both were young men, men who worked by the sweat of their brows. William always thought of cancer as "a terrible thing that happens to other people. I always thought I was immortal because I worked hard all my life. I was the exception." He learned, however, that all men are mortal—no exceptions. "All of a sudden it does happen to you. It just makes you really realize how susceptible people are to it. It can be you, too. Even though you might say, 'Oh it's too bad so and so got that,' next thing you know it's right there!" William's sense of self was defined by his ability to work. When that was taken away, he didn't know what to do with himself—or what to think of himself. "[I've never] been sick before," he said. "What bothers me more, I believe, than anything else, is I just can't do no more what I need to do."

Lee was in the same boat. He dealt with the heartache of incapacity by envisioning a heaven that fit him, where he would no longer be saddled with illness and where he could become productive again. "When my time comes, when God pulls my number, I can go play some racquetball with Him or go do some fishing up there. I don't think that I've been so horrifically bad over my life that I'll go to hell. I think I'm going to heaven. Maybe there's a job up there for me to do. I don't know." They both longed to be whole again.

When we asked, "What comes next for you?" Louise O. replied, "I hope death soon, because to me, it's a very underrated part of life. And being like this is not a whole bunch of fun. We teach our kids . . . something about life and what we do and how we behave . . . but nothing about death, mainly because I guess we don't know. But I think everyone should know that being born is terminal. I hate that word, *terminal*, because everybody's terminal. I don't think children are brought up to understand that and to know that this is a normal process."

We should pause to consider what Louise meant when she said death "is a very underrated part of life." So many of the people we talked with were genuinely "ready to go." Gary indicated an excitement about seeing what's on the other side. "I'm ready to live in a mansion my father has built for me up there, walk the streets of gold, be able to walk up to my dad and say hi to him. . . . I'm close to seein' glory!"

So many times I've heard people say something to the effect of "I just hope I die quickly and without a prolonged illness." Or, "The best option would be to die in my sleep." There are two points to make about this type of thinking. The most obvious is simply that we don't get that choice. Some of us go quickly, some more slowly. But a more interesting question is this: "Are you *sure* you want to die suddenly or in your sleep?"

According to the Christian faith, death is really just a transition from life to life for those who believe. Why, then, wouldn't we want to be totally aware of this incredible miracle? In addition, if we truly believe we will actually experience this moment, won't we live our lives differently?

Most of the people we interviewed for this book were immensely grateful for the time between their terminal diagnosis and death. They used this time to gather people around them and to talk about what really matters in life. They used this time to bring about reconciliation, to give and seek forgiveness, and in general, to put things in order. In essence, they used this time to "pack their bags," and to "unpack their bags." Make no mistake, there was a price to pay for this time, in the form of emotional and, especially, physical pain. But it was clear that almost everyone thought it was worth it, up to a point.

"I had two years of warning," Kenneth told us, "to get my act together, to clean up my life, and hit the highlights a little better. . . . I'm all set."

Harriet was blessed to go into a brief remission after she received her terminal diagnosis. She expressed her appreciation for the time she was given.

> I still have cancer. I could start going the other direction just any day and I know that, but what a wonderful time He's given me. I might even get to Thanksgiving and Christmas one more time with my family. I think it would be the best gift . . . [beginning to cry] because I didn't think I would be here this year and no one else did either. Nobody else ever dreamed that I'd even make it to my birthday. I introduced one of my really good friends to a girl and they were going to get married in October. They just knew I wasn't going to make it to their wedding and they planned to put a big basket of flowers on my pew and not let nobody sit there. Since I didn't die, they had to put the basket up. But I got to go to the wedding. I got to pay for the program for the wedding. I got to be there!

It was all summed up beautifully by Linda who said, "I love life. I love life. I like to laugh. I like to live. But I have gotten to a point that death to me is going to be so wonderful. I look forward to it. I mean, I don't want to get gruesome or anything, but death is not bad if you're ready. That's between me and God and no one else!"

As Richard A. told his story, it was clear that while he was ready to go, he would love to have more time, especially with his family. "I won't even be here on my fifty-first birthday, or see my granddaughter graduate, or even say her first word or get her first tooth. . . . That's where all of this has put me right now. It's kinda to the point that I'm tryin' to relax and see that, hey, this stuff is important, but [I'm learning] what is more important now. You know, I'm learning about things that I don't get uptight about anymore." His comments were reflective of a general message that became apparent throughout these interviews—"the final healing" had already begun in these lives and it was reflected in their recognition of what really matters!

Kenneth also had a strong grasp of this idea of death as the final healing. ALS was wasting his body away little by little, day by day. But he put no confidence in the flesh. All his hopes were fixed on heaven. He was keeping a close eye on his lung capacity, a vital measure of health for patients with degenerative diseases like his. The reason may be surprising. He needed to know when his lung capacity dipped below 30 percent: "At that time I will ask our church to pray for my death." You read that right. Kenneth made a special request of his pastor. When announcing his death, he asked the pastor to tell the congregation, "Great news! Kenneth has gone to heaven."

"You can't get to heaven unless you die," Kenneth pointed

out. And heaven was his only hope for a glorified, perfected body. He longed for the final healing.

Preparing Physicians for Death

The patients, their families, and their friends aren't the only ones who struggle with the initial bad news that medicine has nothing left to offer. Harriet's doctor ordered a bone marrow biopsy as they sought to understand her illness. They hoped for some other, less-serious answers, but they found cancer.

He was on vacation [when the results came back], but he came in [it was New Year's Eve] and called me and told me to bring my family. He's been my doctor for twenty years and he's my parents' doctor, so he knows the whole family. Well, he couldn't tell me I had terminal cancer because he just couldn't do it. So, he told me just enough. [Later] I said, "You're chicken, you couldn't tell me." He said, "I told you all you could handle that day, and all I could handle." He cried when he told me, which is pretty admirable for a doctor. He's very kind.

Traditionally, medical schools have not explicitly helped pre-pare physicians to deal with the issues surrounding death and dying. Vanderbilt Medical Center is helping to lead the way as they now put significant focus on educating the physicians on the is-sues surrounding communication with dying patients and general palliative care—"the active, total care of patients whose disease is not responsive to curative treatment."

In the course of researching and writing this book, I had the opportunity to speak to the Vanderbilt residents on two occasions. The basic message I presented to them is that they will not achieve their full potential as physicians unless they are able to help people learn how to die. While this seems counterintuitive and may not be the first thing we look for when shopping for a doctor, we really believe it to be important.

In the process of meeting with these incredibly bright and highly motivated young people, I asked them a couple of questions I borrowed from Morrie Schwartz (from Tuesdays with Morrie).[3] The first question was, "How many of you know you're going to die?" Every hand in the room went up. The second question was, "How many of you really believe that you're going to die?" A few scattered hands were slowly lifted. "No, you don't!" I challenged, and all but a couple were then lowered. We went on to have the most amazing conversation about the appropriate role of doctors and why it was important for them to reach the point in their lives—now, not later—that they actually believe they are going to die.

Chapter 17

LIVING FOR OTHERS

John was the kind of guy you couldn't help but love. He was mentally challenged, and though he was about fifty, he was like sunshine everywhere he went. And he went a lot of places. He loved trucks of all kinds—delivery trucks, tow trucks, fire trucks, buses—and for most of his adult life he walked or bicycled kind of a circuit in Nashville checking in on the men who drove the trucks he loved so well. He knew all the firemen at several firehouses, as well as policemen, tow-truck operators, ambulance drivers, and Shriners. For several years he rode shotgun with a bread deliveryman, then a milk deliveryman who took a special interest in him.

John once got mixed up with the Secret Service; he joined in the presidential escort when Jimmy Carter was coming through Nashville. Whenever John felt like visiting with the judge, he rode his bike to the courthouse and sat himself in the judge's office. And the judge saw him! John claimed even to have caught a ride to Texas once on Ernest Tubb's tour bus.

It was really remarkable how much people loved John. Busy, hardworking, sometimes gruff men always seemed to have time for him. He had no family, so those men were a family to him. His bread deliveryman friend helped him get social security payments and a place to live. Jack, the milk deliveryman, would take John to run errands or do other things on a regular basis. John's friends gave him their old uniforms; on any given morning, he might be dressed as a fireman, a policeman, an EMT, or any number of different deliverymen. Ernest Tubb saw to it that he got in free at the Grand Ole Opry when it was still in downtown Nashville.

But of all John's many friends, nobody served him more faithfully than Maggie, the wife of Mike, one of his tow-truck-driving friends. John hung around at the towing company for years, and Maggie and Mike took care of him in a great many ways, from getting him out of trouble when he didn't pay his phone bill, to buying him clothes, to taking him to the bank. After several years, John's health began to fail and he found it harder to take care of himself; Maggie and Mike started doing more and more for him. Maggie even cleaned his very dirty apartment on a regular basis.

When cancer caused John to be hospitalized, Maggie spent thirteen days in the hospital with him—eight of those days in intensive care. The hospital made an exception to their visitation policy, given John's special circumstances. When he left the hospital, he came to live with Maggie and Mike and their children. And there he stayed for the rest of his life.

The sacrifices Maggie and Mike made for John were simply amazing. A home-health nurse came once a week, but on a day-to-day basis, it was Maggie who nursed him—sometimes through some very intense situations. They treated John like one of the family, giving him a quality of life and affording him a dignity that wouldn't have seemed possible given his situation.

When we left Maggie's house, Judy and I turned to one another and said, almost simultaneously, "We just saw an angel in there." But Maggie didn't see herself as angelic. In fact, she thought she and her husband and children got more good out of serving John than he got from being served by them. She said, "I say that *he's* an angel because I feel that he's kind of helped us. Even for myself, not to take things for granted, 'I want this,' or 'I want this and I want that.' What I've got is okay."

Maggie told the story of what she learned from John at Christmastime.

I think my kids have learned a lot, not to expect the big things in life but just the little things are just as important. I'll tell you something he did, if I can keep from crying. Christmas morning Santa Claus came and [John] got a stocking and his stocking was a bunch of candy and a little Harley Davidson pin like you put on your shirt and a Shriner pin that has a little diamond in it. He had hair clippers and a new tape measure and that was about it that was in his stocking. [The real gift-opening was going to happen later that afternoon when the rest of the family gathered.] So, after we opened up our stockings and the little one opened a couple of little gifts, I went into the kitchen and was cooking. John came in there to me, "Man, Santa sure was good to me this year." I just about laughed. Two pins! Something that simple was so great to him and he still had twelve gifts to open. He had no idea they were there and didn't even care because that was all he needed.

Maggie wasn't interested in congratulating herself—or being congratulated—for what she was doing for John. She loved him. What more reason did she need for serving him?

People tell me all the time at church and just friends in general, "You're a blessing to John, there's going to be a place in heaven for you," and all those things. But you know, I don't even think of those things. I mean, I do appreciate the comments, and I understand where they are coming from, but they have no idea of the feeling that is there. I don't know why I do it. I don't know why I do, other than I love him.

That's not false humility. Humility—true or false—isn't the issue here. Maggie grasped the truth of Jesus' words: "Whoever loses his life for my sake will find it" (Matt. 10:39 NIV). It's one of the central paradoxes of Christianity: our lives get richer when we give them away. It makes no earthly sense. We nod in agreement when someone says, "It is better to give than to receive." But how many of us are living like we believe it? People like Maggie show us that's not figurative language; it is *literally* true—*demonstrably* true—that it is better to give than to receive. Sometimes it seems we have to be at the extremities of life to see how true it is. As William Wordsworth said,

> *The world is too much with us; late and soon,*
> *Getting and spending, we lay waste our powers.*[1]

Julia was another person who didn't waste her powers on getting and spending. She was a giver all her life. Though she and her husband had the means, they rarely went on true vacations. They only went on mission trips, to serve those less fortunate than they. That may sound like self-denial or perhaps the repression of their own desires. But Julia and Larry both understood that serving others was the one place they could be sure to find abundant life. That's not self-denial; it's good common sense.

As her husband Larry pointed out, Julia's giving spirit was as strong as ever even as she was near to death. He told of a housekeeper who had been coming to their house since Julia became house-bound. He described the housekeeper as "kind of a crusty young girl, not very kind to people." Julia couldn't even speak, but something about the sweetness of her spirit got through to the younger woman. "She's had such an impression on this girl that she brought Julia a lily the other day."

In Julia's case, the impact she had on people wasn't necessarily the result of calculated effort (though thirty years of teaching Sunday school for five-year-olds surely took some calculated effort). So when five or six hundred cards poured in from people telling her what a difference she made in their lives, she seemed a little surprised. According to Larry, Julia said, " 'I never did those things, I didn't help anybody.' She just loves people, and that was the difference. It's what she's always done. That's what years of love and service has been."

A lifetime of selflessness shaped everything about Julia. On the day she received her terminal diagnosis—the day, of all days, when a person might be excused for being self-absorbed or self-pitying or self-indulgent—she was none of those things. As Larry said, "Julia's big question when she came home that day was, how is God—not her—how is God going to get the glory out of my death? The answer came to us over a series of weeks. God doesn't get the glory out of your death; He gets the glory out of your life."

God gets glory out of your life. It's a staggering truth, and it's a reminder that when the terminal diagnosis comes, it's a little too late to *start* living for others. Our interviewees understood, sometimes for the first time, how important it is to live for others. But the real question was, what characterized their lives to that point? Harriet spent her life serving other people. She told an amazing story about a neighbor—suffering from Alzheimer's—whom she took care of for several years. The woman's family wasn't taking care of her, so Harriet took over. The woman had lost her mind so completely that Harriet knew nothing about her other than what other people told her. Yet she faithfully served her. Perhaps we shouldn't have been so surprised, then, to learn that Harriet was still making meals for shut-ins even after she was in hospice care. She was dying of a very painful bone cancer, yet every chance she got she cooked a meal for shut-ins. It was just what she had always done. It was just who she was. "It's [God's] life," she said. "It's not mine. It's God's light shining, but I've always tried to be the one to pep people up."

Kindnesses Received

The soon-departed with whom we spoke especially valued kindness. A big reason was the fact they so depended on the kindness of others. And hospice, of course, creates an environment in which kindness and consideration are elevated to a level you almost can't find anywhere else in our culture.

A couple of conversations revealed how much small kindnesses can mean. Kathleen was a beautiful woman, and her hair was a source of pride. "My hair was long and thick—I had beautiful hair," she said. But she lost it to chemotherapy. "The hardest thing that I had to deal with was the loss of my hair," she said. "Tell me I have cancer, tell me that you don't know what it is, but my hair . . ." When she finally came to grips with it, she prayed, "Okay, Lord, take my hair."

But that didn't change the fact she was self-conscious when her hair came out. The very day her husband, Jerry, shaved the last patches of hair from her head, he dropped her off at Wal-Mart for some shopping. While he was parking the car, she ran into a man coming out—a perfect stranger. "He stopped and he looked at me and he said, 'You know, you are really a beautiful woman.' And I laughed and I said, 'Oh, well, thank you,' and he said, 'No, I really mean it'. . . . I told Jerry that God had just picked me up."

It was a very easy thing for the man to do. He probably had no idea what a huge difference it made for Kathleen to know she was still beautiful, even without her hair.

Kathleen could have related to something Sarah told us. We asked her, "What is the source of your courage?" Her answer was both obvious and deep: "Other people's encouragement." Why yes. Of course. Why didn't we think of that?

Looking back on their lives, it was what people gave, not what they got or spent, that was a source of pride. Abe was most proud of the fact he fought for the independence of the nation of Israel, having left his native South Africa to join the Israeli army. It was one time his actions backed up his life message, which he summarized as: "Love freedom." On the flip side, Samuel was disappointed at his own failure to take part in a similarly big historical event. He lived in Chicago at the time of the 1968 demonstrations, but he didn't participate. He named that as his biggest disappointment.

Charles had been a successful businessman, and he was proud of his business accomplishments as far as they went. But what really made him proud looking back was the fact he was able to use his financial resources to help other people. He gave a lot to charity and to his church. He had two cousins who were disabled for whom he was able to provide in his will. "I'm proud to be able to do it, really," he said. Charles understood what money and success were good for.

Gary, who has made many appearances in this book, was proud of the fact his life changed such that instead of always taking from others, he found himself in a position to give, helping other men through the rehab and spiritual renewal that changed his life: "Now there's other guys getting chances that God gave me. He was able to work through me, use me, and that was an experience I'll never forget."

Vicki's story will be a good way to conclude a chapter on living for others. She was diagnosed with cancer once before, when she was still a young woman. The doctor told her she had six months to live. Vicki can pick it up from here. "I told her, I said, 'I don't think so. You tell me I got six months to live, I'm telling you there's too many people I got to meet, too many places I want to go and too many things I want to see. I got two babies in there that I'm gonna wanna be with. I said it ain't gonna work.'" So for the sake of her children—and for herself, of course—Vicki went through chemotherapy and held the cancer at bay for almost thirty more years.

Vicki spent those years loving people well. She took it as her mission in life to help kids in trouble. So through the years, she took in foster children, both official and unofficial, and adopted one or two children. She laughed, "Most people bring home stray cats and dogs. I bring home stray kids."

She told the story of a fourteen-year-old hitchhiker she picked up in California. The girl said she was going to Hollywood. "This is like the umpteenth hundredth time she'd run away from home," Vicki said. "'You come home with me tonight,' I said, 'get a shower, get a good meal and we'll talk. Get a good night's sleep, and if you still want to go to Hollywood I'll take you. I'll take you tomorrow.' She never left. She's called me 'Mom' for twenty years."

Another time a fifteen-year-old girl she knew was abandoned by her mother, who left town with a man who didn't want any kids tagging along. Vicki took the girl in and gave her a home. Vicki's youngest child was a boy she adopted after she convinced his birth mother not to have an abortion. Vicki was a woman willing to put her money where her mouth was. She really didn't have a lot, but what she had she gave to those children.

"You only live once," Vicki said. "But if you live it right, once is all you need." Her first encounter with cancer caused her to get more serious than ever about what was important in life. Now that she was beyond curing with this second bout, she cried sometimes—but not out of self-pity. "When I cry, I don't cry because I'm scared. I cry because I'm going to miss them so much. That's why I cry. I don't cry because I'm afraid, I cry because I'm gonna miss them." Vicki was the sort of person greedy for life—in a good way. She was determined to live her life to the fullest, which to her meant doing the most good. She was greedy for life after death, too. "I used to be satisfied with things," she said. "I wanted that little tiny—just give me that little corner in heaven, okay? I just want that little bitty corner, that's all I want. Not anymore, honey. I want it all!" If good works are any way to earn extra rewards in heaven, we can be confident Vicki is enjoying more than just one little corner in heaven!

Carol put things in perspective when we asked for her one message she would like to give the world if she could. "We have to live for one another. We're here to help one another along the road. If we lose sight of that, we've lost a lot." Amen.

He Gave It All Away

Jack Logan was our family dentist for many years and, along with his wife, Wanda, taught our Bible study group when we were actually eligible for the Young Couples Class. So it's been awhile. Jack's theology was solid. He was a very smart, avid student of the Bible. But to be truthful, it wasn't the theological lessons that made Jack special. It was his kind, gentle, loving, and sweet spirit. And he was one of the people we always knew we could count on, especially if we needed help. Through the years our respect and admiration for Jack not only endured, but steadily grew. We moved to a different state and only had intermittent contact for several years. But then

I heard some very disturbing "news from home" and went online to see what I could learn.

It seems Jack and others from his Fellowship Bible Church went on a mission trip to Nicaragua. Over the course of the past several years these mission trips had become Jack's passion. After their days of service ended, most of the team returned to the United States, but Jack and his friend Bert Alexander stayed behind to enjoy a couple of days of recreational fishing.

The outing that day was on Lake Nicaragua. At one hundred miles long and forty-five miles wide, this is a big lake. There were ten people on the boat when it was apparently capsized by a large wave. Included in this group was the pastor of a Nicaraguan church, his wife, and three children. The pastor and his wife died almost immediately after the accident and the other eight held on to either the capsized boat or floating debris. Jack, Bert, and two of the pastor's sons held on to a large ice chest that floated and gradually became separated from the others. As the minutes became hours and the hours led to darkness, the four of them held on and paddled, hoping they were headed for shore, but not able to be sure. No rescue came. Throughout the night they became aware of a very disturbing trend; the flotation that the four of them shared and were relying on was beginning to lose its buoyancy. The next day arrived and they found staying afloat was gradually becoming a struggle.

As their energy level began to drop and they became weaker, Jack made a decision. He told the other three what he wanted them to tell his family—what they should say to his beloved wife, Wanda, what they should say to his three sons and their wives, and what they should say to his three grandsons and two granddaughters. And then, he let go of the flotation and swam away.

Later, as the buoyancy continued to decline, Bert Alexander let go and swam away also. The next day, after spending forty-eight hours in the water, the two boys along with the four who had been with the boat were rescued. Jack and Bert had departed.

What a tragic story! But what an amazingly sweet and loving story! As we reflected on what Jack and Bert had done, we were in awe of the courage and the pure, selfless love that was required to do what they did. Imagine yourself in a similar situation—holding on for life, hour after hour after hour, lost, cold, and afraid. Your head tells you something has to be done, but would you even entertain the thought, much less somehow find the courage to take action? In the midst of this situation Jack, and later Bert, acted willingly, deliberately, and purposefully in giving up life with the intent to preserve life for others.

These two boys who survived owe it to Jack and Bert to live meaningful lives and to make a difference in the world by serving others. The value of their lives went up radically because of the lives given up for them. Isn't that what Jesus Christ did, acting willingly, deliberately, and purposefully to redeem others? And didn't that action radically increase the value and worth of each of our lives? And shouldn't I live my life differently out of love for One who would make such a sacrifice?

In his living Jack Logan taught me a lot of powerful lessons as a member of his Bible study class, but in his dying I have been able to see how deeply he was transformed by those lessons. Once again, the words of the Vince Gill and Al Anderson song "What You Give Away" ring in my ears.

Jack Logan and Bert Alexander gave it all away.

Chapter 18

LIVING FOR GOD

In just our second interview we encountered David, a young man dying of AIDS. As previously mentioned, David expressed a very negative attitude toward "religious people" because of the sense of rejection and hurt he felt. When we asked him, "What comes next for you?" he retorted, "Is this a religious book? Because if it is, our interview is over!" We went on to tell him we didn't know if it would be a "religious book" or not—it all depended on what people told us. Now that it's done we still don't think this is a book about religion, but with all the talk about God, Jesus, heaven, grace, love . . . it certainly qualifies as a "spiritual book."

We saw lives being spiritually transformed in the shadow of death. "If anyone is in Christ, he is a new creation; the old has gone, the new has come!" (2 Cor. 5:17 NIV). It was amazing to look into the eyes of the people we talked to in the course of researching this book, and see how true that was. We weren't seeing old, worn-out lives, but new life, as these people got ready to take off mortality like an old coat and put on immortality in its place.

The grace of God did its work on these people—was still doing a lot of work. As people talked about the past, sometimes relating awful things they had done, or that were done to them, it seemed as if they were talking about somebody else. Gary, for instance, talked about the "old Gary"—the one who didn't know Christ—as if he wasn't the same person. And, of course, if you believe what the Bible says, they *weren't* the same people. They were new creatures, just months or weeks or days away from seeing Christ perfect in them the work He began in them.

So when we asked the soon-departed what their message to the world would be, we heard a lot about the importance of living for God, reading the Bible, staying involved in church. Every now and then we got the impression people talked about God because they thought they were *supposed* to. But we also talked to a lot of genuine saints who spoke from the heart.

Christine's testimony was stirring. Here was a person who understood God's grace from the inside out. "The Lord has been so good to me," she said. "He's done so many things in spite of everything I've done. . . . My experience has been when I got myself in trouble over my own foolishness God has been the One who has come and bailed me out." She went on to say that when you find yourself in trouble, "Never run from God—run to Him!" That's the gospel in a nutshell. God does good to us *in spite of* what we've gotten wrong, not *because of* what we've gotten right. We get ourselves in hot water and don't have the wherewithal to get out, but a gracious God reaches in and pulls us out . . . *in spite of ourselves*.

Bear in mind, this person who is talking about all the good things God has done is dying a slow death of emphysema. "Never get the idea when something bad happens that you're being punished for what you've done wrong. That's the devil's territory." Christine had left the devil's territory far behind. There was a time, however, when she found herself in the middle of it. There was a time when she was suicidal.

Her husband of twenty-six years left her for another woman. "I hurt so bad," she said. She waited until the kids left the house, then she went into the shower to slit her wrists. "I worked in nursing, so I knew where to cut," she remarked. "At the last minute, I said, 'Lord, if You're real, please help me.'" And He did. "He showed me in a flash my whole life. And He showed me—in a way that didn't hurt me—where I had missed it. I remember laying on the bed . . . it was an odd little voice, and He said . . . 'I was there before you to save you.'"

Thus began what Christine called her "adventures in faith." She was never the same again. "I was just thrilled that the God of the universe was talking to me."

Christine's husband came back, then he left, then he came back, then he left several times over a two-and-a-half-year period. It was heart wrenching, but it was a key time for Christine to learn to put her trust in God rather than in a man. One day, her husband asked, "'Are you seeing someone?' I said, 'No. Why?' He said, 'You have such joy on your face. You radiate. You must be in love.' I said, 'I *am* in love. Let me tell you His name. His name is Jesus, and you need to know Him.' He just about fell out." It wasn't long before Christine's husband received Christ, too, and came home for good. "It's been one adventure after another," Christine said.

Christine experienced life-transforming grace, and the reality of that experience made her want to tell others. "A lot of people aren't Christians, and I realize that, but I would assure them that Jesus is the most real person you can imagine, and the best thing you can do is to get wrapped up, tangled up, and tied up with Jesus. He'll never let you down."

Not everybody had so dramatic a story as Christine's. But an overwhelming number of people made it clear that their main message to the world was connected to their spirituality. More specifically, they said the way to lead a life that matters was to know and trust God. Most of them pulled no punches, with several delivering short sermons! John H.'s message for his family and the more than one hundred foster children he helped raise along the way couldn't be more direct: "Trust in God. Live life to the fullest." Sarah's basic, straightforward message to her grandchildren was characteristic of what we heard many times: "Stay away from evils, keep away from evil things . . . be good. Live so as to be allowed into His kingdom. Hear the angels sing!" Sarah's theology was simple but powerful, and it came from a woman who was already hearing "the angels sing." We should listen carefully.

Rose R., too, boiled things down as simply as she could: "Be as close as you can to God. Pretty simple, isn't it? Well, if you do that, you're going to live the best you can." Kenneth began his message to the world by saying, "Get right with God. Do what He says; you'll be blessed forever. Is that helpful?" *Pretty simple, isn't it? Is that helpful?* These are a couple of understated questions that actually make a powerful statement! Kenneth goes on to say, "If you don't have God in your life, you're going to have a miserable life." William M. implored the world, "Live your life for Christ and accept Him."

Such straightforward, powerful messages. Sam's entire message ended with a hope that he had figured this out. "Believe that there is a God and try to serve Him. That's the best I can do." My guess is that would be more than good enough.

An evangelistic message was front-of-mind for several of those interviewed. They wanted people to know, especially their children and grandchildren, how important their faith had been to them, and especially wanted them to know how vital it was to them as they lived their final days. Mildred wanted to encourage people to "begin early in your life as you live your life for your Savior. . . . Get started a little quicker!" A quick start to spiritual development was also on the mind of Reitha. "[People] should, early in life, give their heart and their direction of their life to the Lord." The practicality of such an early, efficient start wasn't lost to her either. "And that way they'd be much more helpful to themselves and everyone else."

Lucille's invitation was straightforward enough when she said, "Confess Christ and live for Him. 'Cause there's something better for us up there somewhere. There's somethin' better!" When asked if she had anything to add to the message specific to her grandchildren, great-grandchildren, and great-great-grandchildren she said, "Be a Christian. They'd have more pleasure, and feel safer, be a Christian. Christ says, 'Without Me you cannot enter the kingdom.' He doesn't say you may not. He says you cannot." On a similar, very serious note, Virginia expressed her personal hopes that "we will all get there [heaven] together someday" but then closed with a very authoritative statement: "There's only one God, you know."

The same evangelical fervor comes through in Leon. Here's his message to his grandson: "To find his Savior in life and to believe in his Savior and worship his Savior and it will come to him. That Almighty up there is it and you better have Him when you get ready to go because you're going to need Him. That's what I would say!"

Imbedded in several of these messages is a theme that we will have a better life on earth if we seek God. They're not just talking about life after death, but the abundant life here—the life Jesus promised: "I came that they may have life, and have it abundantly" (John 10:10). These people, having almost lived their complete lives, reported the best living they ever did was when they were walking with God. Maver said her message was, "Well, it's to be a Christian. I think that's the most important thing. I know that I've been happier since I've been in the church than I ever was in my life. I was in the church a long time, but then I wandered away. Then I didn't go back until '82. Then I repented, I guess. I've been faithful to the church . . . but I'd say that's the most important thing—be a Christian." Kenneth's previously stated response shows the other side of the "abundant life" concept. "If you don't have God in your life, you're going to have a miserable life." He emphasizes the importance of the basics—"Read your Bible, find out what it requires of you, [find] a church to help you . . . understand what you read."

Mildred's faith resulted in a settled mind, a hope of heaven that made life on earth that much sweeter. "I mean when I go to sleep, I don't worry anything about it." Anticipating heaven she said, "Of course Mom and Dad are there and all my relatives and my husband is there, so if something happens to me that's fine. 'Cause I know where I'm going."

Living for God means being confident He has all of our affairs in His hands. It means believing He controls everything and He has our best interests at heart. A recurring theme was that people who believe they are in control of things are only fooling themselves. After all, these were people in positions of utter helplessness. If they ever really believed they were "in control," they clearly believed differently now. Calvin K. was an exception. He told us that of all things in his life, the greatest thing he had ever done was "to be the captain of my own spirituality." Almost all of the soon-departed recognized they were in the midst of a rapid physiological decline that neither they, nor anyone else, could control. They also accepted that they would soon enter another process infinitely more unknown and out of their control—death. What are we to do when we can't control things?

Trust, that's what. We heard a lot of talk about trust. Approaching death forces the issue—you either trust or you become frantic or fearful. Once you accept that you aren't in control, trust becomes a very logical choice. The question becomes not *Do I trust?* but *Whom or what do I trust?* Annie made it clear where she stood. "I try to accept that this is something we all have to face and that we all go through it. And you just have to say, you have to just turn it over to the Lord." She went on to say, "First I would say, put the Lord first . . . just trust Him, just trust the Lord." Lena had a similarly strong message about trust: "First, you trust in God. The Scripture says trust in Him with all your heart. That really speaks quite a bit."

We should not overlook that both Annie and Lena began their statements about trust with the word *first*. That's where a lot of people get hung up on trust. You have to trust first, before you know all of the facts and before all of the details are revealed, and maybe most difficult of all, before you know the outcome for certain. That's what the concept of faith is all about—relying on something or someone you can't see, touch, feel, smell, or hear, something beyond the five-senses realm of existence.

Our interviewees' advice to the world suggested that, no matter what direction we turn, we should encounter God. Harriett responded to our question with certainty.

I know exactly what I'm going to say. I used to teach the youth and that's a tough age to teach. I used to tell them, "Live like Jesus was sitting right beside you. Don't do anything you wouldn't do if Jesus was physically sitting right beside you!" I wish I had thought about that years ago myself. But I didn't. I did things foolishly, but I've always encouraged the kids to live like Jesus was in your pocket or in the car with you, at school, at home when you're talking to your parents. I have always encouraged them. So I would tell the world to live like Jesus was right next to you and have Him in your heart so you won't go to hell. I would tell everybody in the world to please come to know Christ. [Sobbing now.] Please. You have to. You don't have to, but if I could tell the whole world one thing, I would say . . . God wants you to live so He'll be proud of you when you get there. "Come on in, you faithful child." That's what I would tell the world.

Here's how Florence responded when we asked her for a message to the world:

I don't know about other people, but here's what I try to tell myself. . . . Sometimes, it gets difficult, particularly as you get older and have real problems. "The rain is going to come today, but the sunshine will be tomorrow." When I would see that rain, the rain in my life, I say, "Well, the sunshine is going to come tomorrow." . . . The second thing I say to myself at night is, "God, walk before me, behind me, beside me, just stay with me." So at night when I wake up [I think], *Why worry at night? Because God is awake.*

If we listen to the voices of the soon-departed, we will surround ourselves with God's presence. We'll "live like Jesus is sitting right beside us." We won't "turn away from God," but will "run to Him," rather than away from Him. And we'll invite God to walk all around us—before us, behind us, beside us—just stay with us!

If William S. sounded like a preacher, it's because he was one. "Well, I guess the message would be to turn to the Lord, because He's got the answers. He's got all the answers. Sometimes they're hard to find, but they're there. They're there. And He will take good care of you if you will allow Him to. Don't turn to the Lord and hold on. That doesn't work. You've got to turn it over to Him. And I can say this because I haven't been the greatest at doing just that, but I will say that I have tried. I would say that's the best thing. Turn everything over to Him and have complete and utter faith in Him and love Him and love your family, particularly, love your family and Him. I think that's probably the most important thing. . . . Love the Lord, love your family, and love other people!"

"I Must Have Done Something Right . . ."

One phrase we heard several times during the research for this book was, "I guess I did something right." Mary T. said she was proud of how her kids turned out. "It made me think I did something right." Sam's kids had turned out well, his wife still loved him, old students from his teaching days still came to see him. "I must have done something right," he said. When Mildred's Sunday school class brought her meals every other day for two months, she took it as an affirmation that she was loved and valued—and an affirmation that "I must have done something right."

It may not be as basic as food, water, and shelter, but the need to feel you've done something right is pretty basic. It was important to "the 104" to know their lives meant something. William E. was close to despair because he felt he hadn't done anything right: he felt he made the wrong choices "probably ninety-nine percent" of the time.

That's why encouragement is so important—and not just at the end of life. Talk to the people around you, and make sure they understand they've done something right.

Shirley was a "star interview." Our conversation with Shirley provided enough information to write a short book just about her. Shirley would have been a powerful preacher, and the day I visited with her, she was. She made it absolutely clear that her life really began when she "found the God of my own understanding—not my daddy's God and not the preacher's God—but the God of my own understanding." And to be clear from the outset regarding "the God of Shirley's understanding," it was God the Father through a very personal relationship with Jesus. The closing portion of her "sermon" that day was enough to inspire an altar call at any house of worship, no matter the denomination.

No matter how much money you got, how much education you got, find the God of your understanding. Because there will come a time that you won't have money, and nobody gonna be to your rescue. God will be there, though. Find the God of your understanding. Because He will give you peace, young and old. I don't care what you got. What does it profit a man if he gains the whole world, and loses his soul? Because the verse says "as you go into this world, you going out of this world." And you gonna need somebody. I know Proverbs says a good friend is better than piles of money. And that [good friend] is God. You can have money and people won't even come, pay people, they still wouldn't come. But guess what? A good friend will always be there for you. . . . And you know what? Today I say: You can find peace. You can find that peace. But you ain't gonna find it in materialistic things. You ain't gonna find it in money. You ain't gonna find it in other people. You can find it in God. And you know, I just saw a little bit of light. A little bit. And each day I go through a storm, that light would get bigger, then bigger. Then another storm come in my life, and I endure, and then that light get that much bigger, and bigger!

How could she be more clear? Find "the God of your understanding," accept the peace that comes with that, and then look for the "little bit of light" that marks the beginning of the adventure. Amen.

The Transforming Power of Gratitude

There's more to gratitude than saying thanks for the good gifts you're given. The habit of gratitude (or the "attitude of gratitude" as it's often called) actually reveals good gifts and blessings you might have otherwise overlooked. To put it another way, gratitude transforms the way you understand your life.

Everybody we interviewed for this book was facing something that is near the top of most people's list of fears: lingering, sometimes painful death. But almost to a person, they focused on the blessings of their situation, and their circumstances—or rather, their experience of their circumstances—were transformed. James B. was pretty typical in the way he talked about his rare (and painful) disease: "It's been tough but the blessing is getting to see everybody, tell everybody hi and good-bye and all that. I take it as a blessing rather than, 'Oh, woe is me, look what cards I drew.' You know, I just don't, I don't feel that way about it."

For Rodney, the experience of a terminal illness transformed the way he saw his entire life. "I never knew before now how truly happy I am," he said. And that recognition of a lifetime of happiness shaped the way he looked at the approaching end of life. "We know what the end is going to be, but we've had so many good years together that it will be peaceful."

For the soon-departed, gratitude didn't just transform the end of life into something beautiful. It made them see the beauty of even the most "ordinary" lives. Rose D. expressed tremendous gratitude for the life she led. We asked her to talk about the most important thing she ever did. She said, "My life was just ordinary, and I can't think of anything outstandingly important." She was proud of her work as a nurse, but she viewed her life as very ordinary. Rose had sense enough to be thankful for (and proud of) simple duties done.

Gary was just about to burst from gratitude. You wouldn't call his job a dream career: he cleaned up after hockey games and other events at an auditorium in downtown Nashville. But it was his first gainful employment in a long time, and he had been extremely proud to be giving back to society rather than being a drain. His nieces only knew him as their uncle in prison, but since he started working at the auditorium he was able to treat them to Disney on Ice and a hockey game or two. "It's just been one blessing after another," he said. But even when cancer took that job away from him, Gary was still thankful. "I've got a group of people that love me now that I never knew existed," he said. How could he complain? He marveled at the changes God had wrought in his life, and looked eagerly for the day when he would open the front door to his own mansion in glory.

Conclusion

IT ALL COMES DOWN TO THIS

So, when it all comes down to it, what really does matter in life and death?

Our desire to do this project began, in large measure, as a personal quest for understanding. We thought our lives were on track, headed in the right direction, on course—choose your own cliché. We thought we knew "what really matters." But it's always good to test our thinking, challenge the process, clear the slate, and see what is revealed. We "wrestled with the angel" at Jacob's ladder before, but how about one more bout to make sure we came away with the right answer?

In seeking the answers to our questions, we decided we would like to do a lot of listening. We are both teachers by profession, so putting the focus on listening represented a shift in style. We also wanted to use our experience in social science research to create a quasi-research approach to finding the answers to our questions.

We decided we wanted to listen to people who were very experienced in living. Our first thought was we would just talk with older people, perhaps finding our subjects in assisted living facilities or nursing homes. But on a tour of the Alive Hospice facility in Nashville, Tennessee, the framework for our project crystallized. Here were people who signed a document that essentially said they would no longer seek a cure for their disease and that their prognosis was six months or less to live. So the concept became not just who lived the longest, but who lived the greatest percentage of their life. With death as an imminent reality, we expected these people would be in a "life review" mode and could tell us what has really mattered to them.

We expected to be impressed by what we heard. Our expectations have been exceeded exponentially; more than impressed, we have been amazed, stunned, stopped in our tracks, and moved to tears on several occasions. We've tried to handle their words—words that became sacred to us—with great care. These words are words of truth, integrity, and genuineness and are deserving of our respect and even reverence. As we've reread their words time and time again, we feel we have come to personally know and love several of these people, even though we spent a very short time with them. It's not unusual now for me to think, or even say, "I wonder what Gary or Beverly or William or Shirley or Harold or Anna would advise?"

This process has accomplished its purpose for the two of us. We've been challenged to grant and seek forgiveness. We have become aware of the need for reconciliation to be a part of everyday life and have taken actions in pursuit of that goal. Our focus on purpose in life has been refined and refocused. We've been reminded to grasp for what really matters in life—people (especially family) and God—and we'll try to continue to let go of the other stuff. We've also renewed our commitment to proactively seeking joy in our lives by going after it rather than waiting for it to happen. We're committed to giving away more of our ourselves and our resources. We know—and almost even believe!—that we're going to die someday.

We think we have a better understanding of death and will be more prepared when our time comes. But most importantly, we feel better prepared to live than before. These people have enriched our lives and taught us much more about living than about dying. There is just a "sweetness" about so much of what they had to say. Partially as a result of my personal aging process (men tend to become more emotional as they age), but mainly as a result of being surrounded by these stories and the aura of the soon-departed, I have written the word *sweet* more in the past six months than in my entire life. I've come to associate a different meaning with the Dave Matthews quote that our son Rob uses often: "Life is short, but sweet for certain!"

All of "the 104" have departed. Most left very soon after our conversations. A few of the departures, especially the young and the middle aged, seemed tragic, but most of them told us they departed having lived a good life, with few regrets.

In her book *Final Exam: A Surgeon's Reflections on Mortality*, Dr. Pauline Chen writes about what she's learned about death, dying, and living from her work. In a recent interview with NPR's Scott Simon she talked about the first time she dissected a human body in medical school. The cadaver was a woman who died of ovarian cancer, and her body's muscles, with the exception of her face, had wasted away. Here's what Pauline Chen told Scott Simon:

> Much of her musculature was atrophied, except for her facial muscles. That struck me, because I had sort of half expected that her facial muscles would be as atrophied as her back muscles. But, in fact, they were more developed. I came to believe—and I do believe—because I've seen this subsequently with patients at the end of life, that my cadaver, in facing the end of her life, ended up living much more fully than the rest of us. And so she probably used those facial muscles—the muscles of smiles, tears— just that much more than the rest of us.[1]

So much of what really matters can be expressed in our face—joy, sorrow, kindness, concern, caring, love, compassion, confidence, peace. After hearing their stories, their words, and their hearts, we have to believe the soon-departed would pass this part of the "Final Exam." We would find their facial muscles in great shape, maybe the best shape of their lives.

Speaking of final exams, we've composed our own final exam for ourselves, and we invite you to accept the challenge for yourself as well, to determine how much we've really learned from the soon-departed. This is what I always like to refer to as the "So What" phase of our learning. We may have heard some interesting, maybe even inspiring stories. We may have even learned some new information and feel more knowledgeable about the subject. But really, so what?

What difference does it make? What are you going to do about it?

We'll call our exam "The Ultimate Living and Dying Test." We need to make a few points as you prepare to consider this exam. First, read all the questions and the final instructions before you begin to write your answers. Second, students often want to know what is going to be on the test. Well, we feel sure it will be a very comprehensive test and that *every-thing* is going to be on the test. Actually, we believe at some level these questions, and probably a lot more, *are* the test! And finally, success on the test is equally achievable by all segments of our society without regard to race, wealth, social status, religion, golf handicap. Everyone has an equal opportunity to pass this test. The only exception is that children do seem to have a fairly significant advantage.

What we were asking are two core questions: "How should we live?" and "How can we be prepared for the absolute certainty of death?" These are really important questions and getting the answers right is, in essence, a life-and-death issue! We wanted to hear the voices of people whose vision has been shaped by a glimpse of death. What did we hear? What did you hear as you read these stories and ideas? Should my life change in some substantial way as a result of what I heard? Should your life change in any substantial way as a result of what you heard?

A few words of instructions, maybe even warning, are in order before you begin this exam. First, a word of warning: this is not an easy exam. It is not a "true or false" or multiple-choice exam. This is an essay exam that requires critical-thinking skills. It also covers every aspect of your life—everything is on the test.

But there are also some appealing aspects to this test. It is, in essence, an "open book" exam and you can use every resource available to develop your answers. You can even look at the work of someone else, and if you want, incorporate it into your answer. As you take the exam you can continue to learn from your experience and the new information that you accumulate during the testing period. And, you can change your answer as you go, even though for some strange reason, maybe pride and arrogance, few test takers take advantage of this feature of the exam.

A significant paradox in the instructions is that there is no announced time limit for taking the exam—you can take all the time you have. But time will expire; we just can't tell you when. And when time does expire, you must turn in your test and depart immediately. The test will be expertly graded on a pass-or-fail basis and there are no re-takes of the exam and there is no appealing the judgment.

Are you ready?

Are you sure?

Pencils up . . .

BEGIN!

And God bless you.

THE ULTIMATE LIVING AND DYING TEST

Can you see how the disappointments and setbacks in life are so minor in comparison to the joys and accomplishments?

Can you see how all of life's events—the good and the bad—have shaped your current status in life?

Whom do you need to be reconciled with so that you will be prepared to depart at any time?

Have you identified your real treasures? How often do you gather them around you?

If laughter served as the measure of the quality of your life, how are you doing?

Could you just "let go and swim away," as Jack Logan did?

What "unfinished business" do you have?

Are you intentional in creating joy in your life and in the lives of those around you?

Do you love God with all you heart, and soul, and mind?

Do you genuinely "love others as you love yourself"?

Do you view other people as "immortals to be" and treat

them in ways that will enable you to look them in the eye and smile with genuine affection when you meet them in heaven?

Do you have peace in your life?

Is gratitude a significant part of your daily expression of life?

Are you prepared for the "final healing"?

A WORD ABOUT ALIVE HOSPICE

The concept of hospice care as a part of our health care system is a relatively new idea. St. Christopher's Hospice, formed in 1967 in southeastern London, was the first recognized organization of its type. The hospice movement is based on the recognition that medical treatment is ultimately limited in its ability to prolong life. Alive Hospice of Nashville was founded in 1975, only eight years after St. Christopher's and only one year after the first hospice began in the United States. In 2006 Alive Hospice served over twenty-five hundred people in their homes or in their residential facilities.

Dame Cicely Saunders, MD, and the founder of St. Christopher's, wrote this about the concept of hospice in 1967:

> A Hospice is "a place of meeting. Physical and spiritual doing and accepting, giving and receiving, all have been brought together . . .
>
> The dying need the community, its help and fellowship . . .
>
> The community needs the dying to make it think of eternal issues and to make it listen . . .

We are debtors to those who can make us learn such things as to be gentle and to approach others with true attention and respect."[1]

The Alive Hospice concept is described on its Web page as emphasizing "palliative rather than curative treatment; quality rather than quantity of life. The dying are comforted. Professional medical care is given, and sophisticated symptom relief provided. The patient and family are both included in the care plan and emotional, spiritual and practical support is given based on the patient's wishes and family's needs. . . . Hospice affirms life and regards dying as a normal process. Hospice neither hastens nor postpones death. Hospice provides personalized services and a caring community so that patients and families can attain the necessary preparation for a death that is satisfactory to them."[2]

At the core of the Alive Hospice service philosophy is a belief that no one, regardless of illness, age, or ability to pay, should have to die in pain or alone.

Until the emergence of the hospice concept just four decades ago, the health care community's mind-set was that we should fight death until the bitter end as we continued to develop drugs and surgical procedures to prolong life. While medical science and practice has found many positive ways to prolong life, the hospice model's growth has been fueled by the recognition in the medical community that a point comes, in some cases, when prolonging life becomes a sort of artificial solution that serves neither the patient nor those who love the patient. All 104 of our soon-departed made the personal decision that they had "fought the good fight," but had reached a place where curative treatments would not succeed.

The most unanimous response in our interviews was re-lated to hospice care in general, and Alive Hospice in par-ticular. Without exception, we heard praise for the hospice experience and for the people who delivered the services. Not one single word of complaint was heard in more than three hundred thousand words in the transcribed interviews! That is a truly remarkable testimony to the concept and the people involved.

William S. said, "We cannot praise Alive Hospice enough. They have been absolutely super. They have been so helpful . . . anything you want, why they will do their best to get it for you. The people that have come out to see us have been su-perb—just great from the first lady who came to interview us right on down. Everyone has been so understanding and I just can't say enough for them." William S. also appreci-ated the basic hospice concept as he went on to say, "Quality [of life] has been a lot better, and one of the problems we've had is trying to convince the doctors about quality instead of quantity. They want to go for quantity and we want to go for quality. One of the great things about hospice is that they recognize the importance of quality and they have been just wonderful."

Leon shed tears as he told us about the people of Alive Hospice. "I have never in my life, I didn't know that there were people that was that way. I didn't know there was people in this world . . . they loved me so much, but how do you face death? That's what I wanted to know. How do you face death? It's rough. It's rough. That was hard when he explained to me what it was and how it was and how you would go. He [the chaplain Gene] talks to us about every week. We began to understand and now I know what to face. And that guy Ed comes, bless his heart, and bathes me and everything like that, puts clean clothes on me. Like I told you a while ago, I just didn't know that there was people in the world that was that kind. It's such a wonderful, wonderful organization. . . . You will not have any pain—on a scale of one to ten of pain right now I got zero!"

One after another the praise for Alive Hospice flowed. Shirley called it "a miracle." Rodney and Dena said, "It's like they're family." And Richard A. said, "They seem to be wonderful people—Debbie, Jill, and the chaplain, Gene." The word *wonderful* was used to describe Alive Hospice and its people by James B., Beverly, Harold M., Thomas D., and others. Harold was seeking a way to help others through his death and had already given instructions that people should send memorial gifts to Alive Hospice rather than buy flowers for his funeral.

Virginia gave one of the most ringing endorsements of all. "I have been very happy here . . . this is now my home and my family. I don't feel depressed. I feel comforted. I feel secure. I feel, I can't say 'loved' because I don't know these people that well yet, but I feel a friendship that is very different from anything I've known before. The people are different." Virginia went on to say again that she's "been very, very happy, and I would give anything if I could come up with an idea or be of some help to get somebody to sponsor hospice. . . . Why can't we get a church? There's plenty of them around that could do something about funding Hospice." In her final days, she was seeking to build on and give back to an organization that meant so much to her. Seeking sponsors and donors for hospice!

As we reviewed the transcripts of our conversations it

became obvious that the soon-departed wanted to send a definite and strong message through our work to every person at Alive Hospice. That message was clearly a heartfelt "Thank You!" but it was really a lot more than that. It was as if, in what could have potentially been their moment of greatest fear and darkness, someone came along and took their hand, comforted them, and provided light so that they could see where they were going. That's enough to make a friend for eternity.

NOTES

Chapter 1

1. Lewis, C.S., *The Lion, the Witch & the Wardrobe.* New York: HarperCollins, 1950.
2. Shakespeare, William, "Sonnet 73."
3. Ragovoy, Jerry and Norman Meade, "Time Is on My Side." *The Rolling Stones: 12x5* (Abkco, October 17, 1964).

Chapter 2

1. "The Living Years." Words and Music by Mike Rutherford and B.A. Robertson. © 1988 Michael Rutherford Ltd., Hit & Run Music (Publishing) Ltd. and R & B A Music, Ltd. All Rights for Michael Rutherford Ltd. and Hit & Run Music (Publishing) Ltd. in the U.S. and Canada Controlled and Administered by EMI Blackwood Music Inc. All Rights for R & B A Music, Ltd. Controlled and Administered by Palan Music America (BMI). All Rights Reserved. International Copyright Secured. Used by Permission.
2. Gill, Vince, "Go Rest High on That Mountain." *Vince Gill: When Love Finds You* (MCA Nashville, June 7, 1994).

Chapter 3

1. McFerrin, Bobby, "Don't Worry Be Happy." Bobby Mc-Ferrin: *Simple Pleasures* (Capitol, 1988).
2. O'Hara, John, *Appointment in Samarra*. New York: Vintage Books, division of Random House.

Chapter 4

1. Claypool, John R., *Tracks of a Fellow Struggler*. New York: Morehouse Publishing, 1974.

Chapter 5

1. Kushner, Harold, *Living a Life That Matters*. New York: Anchor Books, 2001.
2. Kipling, Rudyard, untitled poem from *Just So Stories for Little Children*. Garden City, NY: Doubleday, Page and Company, 1927, page 85. Copyright © Rudyard Kipling, 1900.
3. "Is That All There Is." Words and Music by Jerry Leiber and Mike Stoller. Copyright © 1966 Sony/ATV Tunes LLC. Copyright Renewed. All Rights Administered by Sony/ATV Music Publishing, 8 Music Square West, Nashville, TN 37203. International Copyright Secured. All Rights Reserved.
4. LaPrise, Larry, Charles Macak, and Tafit Baker, "The Hokey Pokey."

Chapter 7

1. "Silly Love Songs." Words and Music by Paul and Linda McCartney. © 1976 (Renewed) MPL Communications Ltd. Administered by MPL Communications, Inc. All Rights Reserved.

Chapter 8

1. O'Neill, Eugene, *Lazarus Laughed*. New York: Boni & Liveright, 1927.
2. "The Way We Were." From the Motion Picture *The Way We Were*. Words by Alan and Marilyn Bergman. Music by Marvin Hamlisch. © 1973 (Renewed 2001) Colgems-EMI Music Inc. All Rights Reserved. International Copyright Secured. Used by Permission.

Chapter 9

1. Lewis, C.S., *The Weight of Glory*. New York: Harper-Collins Publishers, 1980.

Chapter 10

1. Newton, John. "Amazing Grace." 1779.

Chapter 11

1. Peale, Norman Vincent, *The Power of Positive Thinking*. New York: Prentice-Hall, 1956.
2. McKenzie, Alec, *The Time Trap*. New York: American Management Association, 1997.

Chapter 14

1. Bolton, Robert, *People Skills*. New York: Prentice-Hall, 1979.
2. Greene, Graham, *The Heart of the Matter*. New York: Viking Press, 1948, 1976.

Chapter 15

1. Lemmel, Helen H., "Turn Your Eyes Upon Jesus." 1922.
2. Buechner, Frederick, *Godric: A Novel*. New York: Harper-Collins Publishers, 1983.
3. *"The Harris Poll #11,"* February 26, 2003.

Chapter 16

1. Kushner, Harold, *When Bad Things Happen to Good People*. NewYork: Shocken Books, 1981.
2. Claypool, John R., *Tracks of a Fellow Struggler*. New York: Morehouse Publishing, 1974.
3. Albom, Mitch, *Tuesdays with Morrie*. New York: Doubleday, 1977.

Chapter 17

1. Wordsworth, William. "The Completed Poetical Works of William Wordsworth." London: Macmillan, 1924, page 353.

Conclusion

1. Chen, Dr. Pauline, *Final Exam: A Surgeon's Reflections on Mortality*. New York: Knopf, 2007.

A Word About Alive Hospice

1. Saunders, Dame Cicely, M.D., http://www.udumbara zen.org/training.html, last accessed February 12, 2008.
2. http://www.alivehospice.org/about-mission.php, last accessed February 12, 2008.

ABOUT THE AUTHORS

Robert Fisher has served in the roles of university professor, dean, academic vice president, and as president of Belmont University in Nashville for the past eight years. He is a Fulbright Scholar and serves in numerous volunteer roles including serving on the NCAA Division I board and executive committee, on the board of the Nashville Symphony, and as the chairman of the Greater Nashville Area Chamber of Commerce.

Judy Fisher has filled the roles of mother, middle school science teacher, and currently, the campus-wide coordinator of interior construction and external landscaping/lighting at Belmont University. Judy conducted the large majority of the interviews for this project. Judy is active in community service where she serves on several non-profit boards including the American Lung Association, the Nashville Opera, and, most notably, the board of Alive Hospice.